Nader's Raiders

Report on the Federal Trade Commission

by Edward F. Cox

Robert C. Fellmeth

John E. Schulz

PREFACE BY

Ralph Nader

GROVE PRESS, INC., NEW YORK

CONTENTS

[iii]

CONTENTS

PREFACE

Before this student task force report on the Federal Trade Commission was issued in January, 1969, Commissioner Philip Elman of the FTC used to complain that one of his agency's biggest problems was that no one was interested in it. This lack of interest developed over the decades from the Commission's wooden, somnolent concept of its statutory mission. On paper, the FTC was the principal consumer-protection agency of the Federal government. As such, the Commission could have been an exciting and creative fomenter of consumer democracy. In reality, the "little old lady on Pennsylvania Avenue" was a self-parody of bureaucracy, fat with cronyism, torpid through an inbreeding unusual even for Washington, manipulated by the agents of commercial predators, impervious to governmental and citizen monitoring.

Throughout its history the Commission has excelled in avoiding monitoring—or, as it is often called, "oversight." A Hoover Commission report, a law review study, a secret Civil Service Commission report—all failed to have any significant impact in the post-1950 period. With political antennae of considerable sensitivity, successive FTC chairmen have placated the Congress by servicing requests of its key committee chairmen, providing them with exclusive information for public release and attention, and cajoling the better of them through a variety of delaying techniques admirable only for their ingenuity.

These political skills reached their most intense application under the chairmanship of Paul Rand Dixon, whose eight-year tenure was scheduled to end in September, 1969. Having spent his career at the FTC, beginning in the 1930's, with an interval in the late 1950's as general counsel to the Senate Antitrust Subcommittee, Chairman Dixon has comforted and charged key senators and congressmen even to the extent of opening in 1968 an FTC office in Oak Ridge, Tennessee, headed by a friend of Representative Joe Evins, who is chairman of the House Appropriations Subcommittee, which votes funds for the Commission. He faithfully dunned agency officials for contributions to the Democratic party, listened attentively to signals or calls from the White House, and assiduously cultivated powerful trade interests by disseminating the myths that most large businesses are honest and law-abiding, that the problem is the few unscrupulous hucksters who give industry and commerce a bad image. In the meantime, he held a tight rein on other FTC Commissioners and the agency—tighter than any other chairman of a Federal regulatory agency. Not only were powers highly centralized in the chairmanship, but Chairman Dixon also refined the art of usurpation of residual powers and authorities. For example, he unilaterally appointed all the top officials of the Commission—some sixty in all—without consultation or sharing his decision with the other four Commissioners. These Commissioners were allowed to participate in naming only the top seven Commission officials—after Chairman Dixon had nominated them.

As the tide of consumer dissatisfaction rose in the 1960's, the FTC droned on, seemingly oblivious to the billions of dollars siphoned from poor and middle-class consumer alike by deceptive practices hiding shoddy and harmful products and fraudulent services. The Commission's vast information-procurement powers were little used. Hearings were rarely conducted, and never were the transcripts printed. Empirical studies of grass-roots business practices, especially in the urban slums, were nonexistent until 1968. Moreover, the Commission's enforcement policies were ridiculous. It did not have and did not actively seek from Congress powers of temporary injunction or criminal penalty. It almost ignored the enforcement tools that it did have. The strongest of these is the cease and desist order, which merely chastises a culprit company after it has pocketed millions with impunity. And before the Commission invokes even this mild sanction, it is willing to accept profuse assurances of voluntary compliance. This process creates delay and encourages the offender's attorneys to create further delays. Cases of unadulterated thievery have stretched on and on before being resolved, while the offender reaped profits never to be returned and devised new schemes not covered by the cease and desist orders.

Recently, the J. B. Williams Company has been under a cease and desist order for deceptive advertising of Geritol. Twice the FTC has warned the company that it was violating the order. For some reason, the Commission's lawyers were reluctant to forward the case to the Justice Department for prosecution. That reason was largely the powerful Washington law firm of Covington & Burling, in which Thomas Austern is a senior partner. Austern's associates would provide the Commission with arguments and with suggested language, and would plead for further consideration of their client's case. Covington & Burling and its client have little to lose by these delays (even after being cited for violations of the order) and much to gain—continuing sales to people misled into believing that Geritol can make them healthier.

Chairman Dixon's agency has avoided many enforcement problems by avoiding the process of detection.

Massive frauds, for example, in home improvements, magazine sales, credit, and sales-promotion games go unnoticed. Only under public criticism and the occasional prodding of Senator Warren Magnuson's Senate Commerce Committee has the FTC acted against some of these. But the Commission is so constituted—because of its high-level cronyism and inadequate personnel and recruitment policies—that these efforts could not get past the symbolic, public-relations stage.

The degree to which documented deceptions are permitted to continue without Commission action is most serious. For years, the FTC has done nothing with its knowledge of the widespread sale of *used* Volkswagens *as new* by nonfranchised dealers. For almost two years it did nothing about Firestone's advertising that its wide-oval tires could stop "25% quicker," despite Commission rules about just such ads. In June, 1969, the FTC issued a press release stating that after a thirty-day period, it would challenge deceptive tire advertisements. But for years it has had the authority and obligation to move against such deceptions. Why was it necessary to issue a release to tell the industry that it would shortly start enforcing the law? Because the Commission was systematically not enforcing the law—a practice that has become its trademark. The FTC has routinely allowed grossly deceptive advertising campaigns to run their course unmolested; and has then been able to declare the matter moot when questioned about inaction.

In the rare instances when the Commission does try to act forcefully against strong economic-political interests—such as with its cigarette-advertising proposals in 1964–65—it finds itself without a consumer constituency and is promptly overwhelmed by the industry concerned. Thus, a Federal agency that should have a strong grass-roots constituency is deprived of this democratic support in large part as a result of its past ineptness and lassitude.

This was the FTC that greeted the students when they began work in the summer of 1968. The surface clues were telling enough—leisurely morning and afternoon coffee breaks, during which elevators to the cafeteria are so jammed that the Commissioners have to use the stairs to get around the building; long lunch periods to permit time for shopping; extended reading of the afternoon newspapers prior to early departure for home as a routine for more than a few FTC lawyers. A 1,300-man agency, including some 500 lawyers, with an annual budget in the neighborhood of $17 million should have little fat and water in its operations, especially considering the challenges this particular agency should meet.

The word that a group of law students was studying the Commission's consumer-protection performance spread rapidly throughout the hierarchy. The Commission employees who were interviewed were almost always polite, but not very informative. Nonetheless, little by little the students began to piece together patterns of behavior that added up to colossal default, demoralizing of younger staff members, and rampant sinecurism for those who remained. By what was lacking, the students came to understand that a reformed Commission could achieve constructive objectives, and from this realization came an optimism that outlasted their dismay. By their persistent questioning and interaction, they formed an indelible understanding of the kind of professional citizenship that would be required for a steadfast, public-interest Commission. In short, unless there can be external professional advocates for consumer interests, even the most fundamental changes in the personnel and procedures of the Commission cannot produce the needed results. A countervailing force in the private sector against the special interests and lobbyists is a vital condition if a regulatory agency is to perform its task well.

By the end of the summer, Chairman Dixon had shown that he did not appreciate the continued presence of the students. Although they took up an infinitesimal portion of the staff's time (and stimulated the staff's thinking), he employed this pretext to direct his subordinates to grant no more interviews and to refer all requests to the office of the Chairman. He added that any further requests for information would have to be rendered in writing to that office, thus severely restricting and delaying access to the agency. Fortunately, an exchange of letters I had with the Chairman led him to reconsider his position. But his hostility was evident when the students returned to Washington in November, 1968, to testify before the Commission during hearings on improving its consumer-protection activities. Two months later, when this report was issued, he reacted with more heat than light in a public statement denouncing the students' report and the students themselves, and avoiding the main issues they raised.

It was Chairman Dixon's behavior that taught the students about the importance of individual characteristics in bureaucratic environments. They had learned about structure, procedures, pressure groups, and other depersonalized dynamics in their university and law-school courses. But the social and legal studies in the universities do not grapple with the personal dynamics of bureaucratic-system leaders. This is not the case with Washington's lobbyist-lawyers and others who distinguish between form and substance. When they wish to detain or obtain Commission action, they bring their knowledge of the commissioners' preferences, concerns, weaknesses, and alliances into highly strategic and effective play. They take the same approach to officials down the agency hierarchy. Aware as they are of their procedural and legal tools, these lawyers value more the personal and political leverage that operates unrecorded and subvisibly within and without the agency's infrastructure. Procedural and other legal tools are tactics of last resort, to be deployed only after the conflict descends to the formal, relatively open, administrative process. It is then that cumbersome procedures can be used to delay and produce the attrition that results in more advantageous concessions by agency officials. As one corporate lawyer once told me, "The last thing I want for my client is administrative due process." For irregularities in formal procedure offer technical opportunities for such corporate counsels to appeal to the courts to overrule the agency's decision—a prospect that further discourages an agency with limited resources.

The release of the students' report coincided with the change of Presidential administrations. With a different political party in the White House, political factors would undoubtedly result in the replacement of Paul Rand Dixon as Chairman. The only apparent response to the students' report and the resultant commentary by the Nixon Administration was the appointment of a committee comprising 16 lawyers and economists, under the auspices of the American Bar Association, to investigate and recommend improvements for the FTC. This report was scheduled for completion by the end of the year.

In the meantime, the FTC did step up some of its initiatory activities in consumer protection that the students covered in their report. (The report does not deal with the antitrust responsibilities of the Commission.) A TV advertising inquiry was set under way; a hearing on the advertising of automotive prices was scheduled for September, 1969, on highly controversial abuses; and several Commissioners were urging the Chairman, with some success, to be less secretive in the agency's information policies. Congress also took an interest in the FTC. Senator Abraham A. Ribicoff held hearings in March, 1969, at which the students presented extensive testimony. Senator Edward M. Kennedy began preparing an inquiry as chairman of the Senate Subcommittee on Administrative Practice and Procedure. Reports from FTC Commissioners highly critical of their own agency were forwarded to that Subcommittee.

It may be that the students have set up a model for young citizen inquiry into the operations of government agencies and the pressure-group hothouses in which they exist. The students seemed to learn a great deal about the regulatory process that could not be learned at law school. Returning to the campus, they found their perceptions deeper, their skills for analysis refined, and their stimulation of fellow students and faculty members encouraging. From their conversations, it appeared that their view of the legal profession's horizons were broadened, and they could see the potential of developing career roles for full-time public-interest lawyers.

During the summer of 1969, more law students would be on their way to Washington to study more agencies— this time with the participation of medical and engineering students. In short time, this scrutiny should extend to state and local governments and other significant institutions. I believe that we may be seeing a social innovation that will produce just and lasting benefits for the country as these young people generate new values and create new roles for their professions.

RALPH NADER

June 4, 1969
Washington, D.C.

NADER'S
RAIDERS

"Nader's Raiders," Summer of 1968

THE AUTHORS

Edward F. Cox: Bachelor of Arts degree, Princeton University, 1968. Special student in architecture at Yale University.

Robert C. Fellmeth: Bachelor of Arts degree, Stanford University, 1967. Second-year student at Harvard Law School.

John E. Schulz: Bachelor of Arts degree, Princeton University, 1961. Bachelor of Laws degree, Yale Law School, 1968. Assistant Professor of Law, University of Southern California.

THE REST OF THE TEAM

Judy Areen: Bachelor of Arts degree, Cornell University, 1966. Third-year student at Yale Law School.

Peter Bradford: Bachelor of Arts degree, Yale University, 1964. Bachelor of Laws degree, Yale Law School, 1968. Special assistant to Governor of Maine.

Andrew Egendorf: Bachelor of Arts degree, Massachusetts Institute of Technology, 1967. First-year student at Harvard Law School.

William Taft IV: Bachelor of Arts degree, Yale University, 1966. Third-year student at Harvard Law School.

AT THE START of June, 1968, seven volunteers who were to be dubbed "Nader's Raiders" by the Washington press corps straggled into the capital from several campuses. Each in his own way had become acquainted with Ralph Nader and his work on behalf of the consumer. One had participated in a seminar Nader had conducted at Princeton University. Some had heard him speak at their law schools and approached him afterward or wrote to explain their desire to work with him. Others had never met him personally, but believed that the usual run of summer jobs for law students (like interning for one of the "top ten" firms in New York) would be less relevant, even though more lucrative, than whatever employment Mr. Nader might be able to provide in Washington.

As students at Harvard, Yale, and Princeton, we had nothing of the reformer in our backgrounds. One of our number was the great-grandson of President William Howard Taft. Another had taught for five years at the exclusive Groton School.

None of us had had extensive exposure to the realities of the Washington bureaucracy.

It was a long step for us in many ways, not least in the physical sense, going from the rich and varied, sometimes comical, architecture of our campuses to the stultifying "civic" architecture of Washington. If there is anything in the theory that the external esthetics of a building reflects its internal essence, then the architect of the Federal Trade Commission building had a genius for sensing the mediocre. The structure sits upon a triangular block at the junction of Pennsylvania and Constitution Avenues, inelegantly set down between the National Archives and the National Gallery of Art. The choice offices occupied by the Commissioners in the rounded "prow" of the building offer a view of Capitol Hill, which serves as a continual reminder to the FTC of the limits to its role as an "independent regulatory commission." The building's granite base, limestone superstructure, and tile roof echo an unimaginative pattern of continuous horizontal lines.

Inside, the building is similarly undistinguished. On each floor long corridors walled in green marble form an uninterrupted triangle. The offices on one side of the corridor look out onto the avenues; the offices on the other side enjoy an excellent view of a triangular concrete courtyard. There is virtue only in the simple-mindedness of the plan—compared with the intricate corridors of the Pentagon or the Rayburn House Office Building, where one can wander lost and confused for hours.

We knew something of what we would find inside the FTC building. It provides office space for the five Commissioners and some 319 attorneys, with secretarial and clerical help. The Commission has 155 other attorneys at field offices in Atlanta, Boston, Chicago, Cleveland, Kansas City, Los Angeles, New Orleans, New York, San Francisco, Seattle, and Falls Church, Virginia, and in the suboffices at Houston and Oak Ridge, Tennessee. The work of these lawyers falls into one of six major bureaus—Field Operations, Restraint of Trade, Economics, Deceptive Practices, Industry Guidance, and Textiles and Furs. (We were to deal mainly with the last three because their work most directly affects the consumer.) Except for the bureau chiefs, the entire FTC staff hierarchy—including the Chairman, his assistant, one of the Commissioners, the Executive Director, the General Counsel, the Program Review Officer, the Comptroller, and the Director of the Office of Administration—occupies the top or fifth floor of offices.

This bureaucracy traces its history back more than half a century. It was in 1914—the year also of the Clayton Antitrust Act—that the FTC was created to regulate "unfair methods of competition." This was a time when rugged individualism still held a high place in American political thought. The credo *caveat emptor*—let the buyer beware—was sacred in the Congress and the courts.

But the Depression revised—even radicalized—America's social thinking. At the highest levels there was dismay over the widespread and dangerous deceptions suffered by consumers. In 1938—the year also when the present FTC building was finished—the Wheeler-Lea Act amended the original statute, giving it some "teeth." It specified that "deceptive acts and practices" were illegal, and it gave the Commission new enforcement powers to deal with violations. Since then, a whole battery of specialized laws—the Flammable Fabrics Act of 1953, the Fair Packaging and Labeling Act of 1966, and others—have made clear the intention of the Congress: It is the FTC's role to bear a primary responsibility for protecting the consumer.[1]

Now, thirty years later, according to all available information, the Commission was not fulfilling that role. Our first task upon arriving in Washington was to examine that information in the light of real experience. We brought with us a college-bred naïveté, which led us to assume that the FTC—public-spirited an agency as it was supposed to be—would open itself to a rigorous scrutiny.

Instead, we ran into a bulwark of bureaucratic defenses and evasions. Even simple documents became elusive. One of the first things we needed was a personnel chart, showing the number of FTC employes and their job classifications. At first the Director of Personnel denied that any organization chart existed. When we learned that the agency's budget-control records contained the necessary information, he protested that these were not public documents, because they contained the salaries of all personnel. Our arguments that the salary information could be easily expunged were ignored. Only when we submitted a written request—as a preliminary action to a court suit under the Freedom of Information Act—were the records released. We were careful to spec-

---

[1] See Section 1 of the Appendix for a brief overview of the Federal Trade Commission.

ify "without salaries" in our request. Yet the Commission did not even bother to delete that "sensitive" data.

We expected that we could learn much from interviews, hoping for an honest give-and-take. Our hopes for such conversations with FTC upper-staff members were disappointed at the outset. Attempts at frank dialogues degenerated into simultaneous monologues—the interviewers pressing for facts, the interviewees responding with generalizations. In his first interview, one of our project members asked an assistant bureau chief for the approximate number of attorneys in his bureau. The official replied that the request would not be considered unless placed in writing. He would consent to speak only on the legal history of his bureau and not about its present operations. Moreover, he refused to speak at all until another attorney had arrived to witness what turned out to be an inconsequential conversation.

We soon found in all our interviews this same insistence on having two attorneys from the Commission present at all times. Although it is tempting to explain this as a need for group reinforcement of individual security, a more basic reason existed. Apparently, any staff attorney that we interviewed alone became suspect in the eyes of his colleagues and superiors.

A veteran FTC reporter explained to us that a tacit yet institutionalized fear—radiating outward from the Chairman's office—pervaded the entire staff. Younger attorneys no longer with the Commission corroborated this with stories of harassment by superiors for real or imagined transgressions of the FTC's oath of secrecy. One such unfortunate had been seen talking to one of us in the halls of the FTC. His division chief warned him to be careful because "the FTC was back on its heels under criticism." As a result he canceled a prospective interview —and not long thereafter found employment outside the agency.

Despite such pressures, some of the younger attorneys were willing to give frank interviews, but only under controlled circumstances and usually outside the Commission. Invariably, they prefaced even the mildest critical statements with warnings of future denials if the source were identified. Still, this is how we got some highly valuable material.

As we began to learn how to obtain useful information, Chairman Paul Rand Dixon imposed an illegal and unprecedented "lockout," forbidding all staff members to communicate with us. In Mr. Dixon's own words (in a letter to Ralph Nader, dated September 13, 1968):

On August 15, I expressed to Mr. Schulz and Mr. Cox my feeling that by then they had had ample opportunity to complete their interviews with our personnel, and informed them that after August 23 they would no longer have unlimited access to staff members. . . . At about the same time I had our staff orally instructed to this same effect . . . I see no reason for rescission of the action I have taken and, considering all the circumstances, I do not believe it will operate to impede the completion of any legitimate study of the Commission or its activities.

Since any member of the public may talk to government officials as long as the official himself agrees, Chairman

Dixon had only the power of institutionalized fear—now supported by a verbal threat—to enforce his edict.

A few of the younger attorneys still consented to be interviewed, but most, including all the bureau chiefs and the acting General Counsel, declined to talk. Their secretaries invariably came back with the reply that an interview with any member of the staff had to be "cleared first with Chairman Dixon."

Fear is an effective organizational glue when all else fails. We would have liked to find that, instead of fear, the Federal Trade Commission had a strong set of motivational goals to claim the allegiance of its staff. Clearly, protection of the consumer and vigorous enforcement of antitrust laws are goals to inspire the young lawyers of a socially conscious generation. Although these are the goals outlined for the agency by law, our probings revealed that the FTC had lapsed into a lethargy that would have been uncovered long ago if it were not for the Byzantine defenses that disguise its everyday activities.

Our collective naïveté proved to be our strength: the more we were hampered in finding what we wanted to know, the more we persisted. When we were called to testify in the spring of 1969 before the Senate Subcommittee on Executive Reorganization, Senator Abraham A. Ribicoff of Connecticut remarked:

> Bureaucracy being what it is, I am fascinated by your ability to get in so deep, and get so much information. I am sure that you gentlemen are the envy of the large number of reporters here.

This book is a revised and expanded version of our report, released on January 6, 1969, which was exclusively the product of the people who participated in the project. We hope it will be a prototype for similar studies by other students. But our debt to Mr. Nader is large. He brought us together and defined the limits of our task. When we became entangled in analyzing the myriad relationships at the core of Washington's bureaucracy, his expertise and knowledge of informative sources kept us moving. Not least, his unpretentious sense of moral purpose encouraged us during the long hours of research necessary for any work of this kind.

II

THE CRISIS

> *Unfair methods of competition in commerce, and unfair or deceptive acts or practices in commerce, are declared unlawful.*

> § 5(a)(1)

> *The Commission is empowered and directed to prevent persons, partnerships, or corporations . . . from using unfair methods of competition in commerce and unfair or deceptive acts or practices in commerce.*

> § 5(a)(6)

The Government and Advertising

THERE HAVE traditionally been three major arguments against government interference with advertising. First, is the argument by business interests that the "perfect" or all-wise consumer cannot be deceived. Second, there are appeals to free speech and subsidiary interests, such as the desire for imaginative and esthetically pleasing ads. Third, there is a general feeling by some that the problems that do come up are unimportant, unreal, or will go away.

The first argument is used most persistently by corporate giants to justify the system and their own activities, but their ads reveal their true estimation of the "omniscient" consumer. Briefly, he is an insecure, sex- and affection-starved paranoid neurotic with an attention span of 10 seconds. Even if today's consumer is capable of understanding the complexities of, say, comparative reliability characteristics of standard automotive engines —which industry moguls pretend he is—these moguls will not give him that information. Instead, they prefer to sell sex and power, in the form of phallic symbols, undu- lating women, and potent wild animals.

The second, or free-speech, argument is admittedly valid. There is a competing interest in favor of the free exercise of communications media and indeed in favor of diverse and clever ads. But when communications are exercised for deception—that is, the deliberate creation of an impression that does not represent the performance of the product—there is no substantial claim of competing value. Larceny by deception has been a crime for many years at common law. There is little free-speech interest in the right to say "your money or your life"; nor is there much in the right to say "if you give me x dollars I'll give you y object," fully intending and subsequently deliver- ing an inferior or dangerous z object. As for the more subtle trends evolving within advertising—sadism, ag- gression, violence—they present questions of ultimately perhaps the greatest importance.

The third, or why-bother, argument minimizes the im- portance of deceptive-practice problems. But, in light of the evolution of modern society, these problems must not be underestimated. It is easy to dismiss the matter with smug self-assurance, saying "no one could be fooled by that." True, if a false claim is apparent, it fails to deceive and is ignored. But if the deception is successful it is often not discovered at all. Even when the product is deficient or dangerous, the faults are often not easy to trace to a specific deception. How is the consumer to know if a given product caused his teeth to decay earlier than they might have otherwise, or his heart to fail earlier? Further, it is particularly hard to detect the deception when a claim is made about the products of competitors, where the consumer is not likely to make direct comparisons. How many will buy two sets of tires to see if one stops "faster" as claimed? Finally, it is easy to make small lies of omission or implication that generate great market advantage and attract little attention.

It is foolhardy to minimize the effect of these practices, for they force competitors into the same practices, and unless there is some agency to test or check the claims they threaten general promotional credibility to the detriment of everyone (particularly of the honest businessman and the consumer). This phenomenon of indifference is found in thousands of American consumers —largely, the college-educated. They increasingly regard advertising as pure bunk. However, because advertising is the only source of information to the consumer about many of the products he buys, and because he is unable to understand, much less pretest them, the increasing cynicism is dangerous. Perhaps it is even more dangerous than the successful deception put over on the majority of consumers, who still believe what they hear. The "Why should I care—I know they're all lies anyway" attitude means the acceptance of an intolerable market condition. It means the surrender of any expectation of truthful information about the products one buys—and of the ability to make demands.

The New Marketplace

Throughout this book we will be showing that we cannot afford to use these arguments, that we cannot accept the damaging aspects of some irreversible and continuing trends that are in effect in our economy today.

1. The rise of the corporate state through the growth of conglomerates and shared monopolies into an oligopolistic structure. The result has been a new type of price fixing, "price leadership." Other accompanying phenomena include interlocking empires, tacit agreements not to challenge mutual vested interests, corporate domination of regulatory agencies, manipulation of credit, and other subtle forms of coercion that block new competitors and new ideas.

Product fixing is beginning to replace price fixing as a central method of avoiding competition. In product fixing, competitors agree to limit the development or characteristics of their products in order to increase sales and profits. The result is planned obsolescence in many products, appliances and clothes especially, which require the purchase of a new product or high repair costs. It is no accident that the automobile manufacturers charge incredible prices for replacement parts. Product fixing is reflected in tacit agreements to limit advertising. Thus, there are few claims in auto ads about safety or other features that would spur competition for items not as profitable as light gimmicks, useless air spoilers, or meaningless racing stripes.

Perhaps the most important feature of the new economy is growing concentration. In an oligopolistic economy, where competitors within each industry manufacture similar products, the consumer will not learn anything negative about any product type. No manufacturer will advertise against his own product type, and no one will advertise against a product not competing with his own. The result is a glut of information regarding contrived distinctions between identical products, but a dearth on their drawbacks.

Cigarette ads are a classic example. Rarely do you hear about the disadvantages of mouthwashes (which many dentists say irritate the mucous membranes of the mouth), detergents (most of which now build up—rather than remove—particles in your clothes, and many of which can irritate the skin), cars of all types, drugs of almost every variety, deodorants (which now clog pores to promote the magic of "dryness"), "brightening" toothpastes (which contain abrasives), diet soft drinks (which can harm internal organs), and so on. There is increasing danger in the type of deception that omits information relevant to the health or safety of a product—particularly those products that harm without warning or through the slow and stealthy destruction of organs.

2. The communications revolution, including use of nationwide television and the rising cost of access to this public forum. This development has made it possible for

businessmen to perpetrate fairly blatant frauds or deceptions, bilking large numbers of people of a small amount in a short time without feeling any significant market check. The recent chinchilla ads on TV provide an example. Another example is the extremely efficient TV chopping and grinding demonstrations involving a number of products that are purchased by mail and whose performance is almost invariably far inferior to what is represented. Indisputably, it is now easier than ever to reach large numbers of people with more subtle forms of influence.

3. The information explosion, including increasing use of mass data-handling techniques to attack the privacy and autonomy of the consumer. This trend has made possible social-psychological analysis of potential markets. Market researchers have divided and subdivided the market along lines that make possible special appeals to different social groups. Most of these appeals are based on distinctions that have nothing or very little to do with the products themselves, but are associated with them to produce "empathy." Virginia Slims are marketed to appeal to feminists, Camel cigarettes to appeal to the he-man, Lark to the suburban set, and so on.

4. The growing sophistication of the science of applied psychology, involving influence by suggestion, subtle deception through image manipulation, and the creation of demand through associations with sex, fear, and power fantasies. A glance at the mouthwash, deodorant, and even dish detergent ads shows the fear approach at work. Meanwhile, the auto ads play upon both power and sex. Sex alone is the basis—usually the *sole* basis—for one-third

or more of all television advertising. The recent advances in motivational research facilitate subtly effective appeals and unapparent deceptions. Some of these seem ridiculous when directly explained, but nothing testifies to their effectiveness more than their consistent success. Not only do businessmen enroll the most accomplished psychologists in the academic world to appeal to the public's fears and frustrations in almost psychotic association attempts, but they also experiment increasingly in more direct forms of forced persuasion, as in the microsecond flashes of Aqua Velva lotion or in the hypnotic waving of keys in front of the screen during the Fairfax Plymouth ads in the Washington, D.C., area with the accompanying deep voice intoning over and over, "you *will* buy a Plymouth at Fairfax Motors."

Past experience suggests that healthy business competition is necessary in a successful economic system based upon private ownership. Indeed, the concept has become one of our sacred shibboleths. In view of the trends we have just briefly noted, however, it is no longer wise or efficient for government to rely solely on fostering competition to do the job. Government must now begin to direct its energies toward active protection of legitimate consumer interests as well. Minimally, this means guaranteeing that consumers obtain adequate information about products available in the market (this should probably include some control over the types of sales approaches that constitute overpowering appeals to strongly irrational elements of the human psyche), and making certain that all consumer products are safe for consumption when reasonably used.

The Old Deceptions

We have only to survey the consumer situation in recent years to realize the critical need for something to be done. The increase in deceptive practices in advertising is manifest throughout the trade. It is clearly a rising phenomenon with more current abuses than any single person or group could document fully.

• Take, for example, the practice of relabeling substantially old products as "new," which with every successive ad campaign has made the word meaningless. Detergents are particularly guilty of this transgression. The current rage here is the promotion of "micro-enzyme action." Our researches, as well as tests by the Consumer's Union (see *Consumer Reports*, January, 1969, p. 44), reveal very little difference if any between the "enzymatic" magic of the Axion or Biz pre-soaks and the results from plain detergents. The only usefulness the process has at all is from sustained overnight pre-soaks for certain specific, rare stains. This does not prevent Colgate or Procter & Gamble from spending millions to advertise a product that then costs double the already inflated price of other detergents. Not only do ordinary detergents have substantially the same pre-soaking powers as the enzyme pre-soaks, but also the new breed of emerging enzyme detergents for wash *per se* (Gain, Tide XK) will have absolutely *no* effect on detergent effectiveness. (Even for the mild and occasional difference the enzyme presoak process makes, the substance must interact with the clothes far longer than the half hour to an hour of a normal wash cycle.)

What will happen when someone develops a truly new process in this or any other field? It is becoming apparent that few will believe it. It is also becoming apparent to many that all the consumer is purchasing from Procter & Gamble, Colgate, and Lever Brothers are the lies he is told about the product. There is little doubt that toothpastes, mouthwashes, deodorants, cleansers, soaps, detergents, and so on are priced between five and twenty times their cost of production. The American people must eventually grow tired of paying $1 for a tube of toothpaste that costs no more than 15 cents to make. It is these purchases that rob the American people of billions of dollars every year. Each one may be small, but they offer an incredible percentage take for manufacturers. This is not to imply that all of the difference goes into profits or mysterious Swiss bank accounts. High corporate profits of 15 to 25 per cent are not so objectionable as the 40 to 50 per cent of the product price that is spent on inherently deceptive advertising. The advertising does not concern truly *new* advances in technology or enhanced qualities of the given product. It employs the invention of empathy mechanisms and contrived distinctions among products that are in reality identical. This is what Americans are paying billions every year for —to be told that there are distinctions where there are none, to be told that products are new when they are not new. In short, the ever-tolerant and deceived American consumer is paying the people who lie to him—for lying to him.

Home and cleansing products are not the only ones guilty of these transgressions. It is a phenomenon that has spread throughout the economy. Every year we are sold so-called new cars, appliances, and other product types. The hope is that we will throw away our present models for the new ones with the additional inch of chrome or the new name or label that conjures up exotic and compelling images. Of course, we may be throwing away a product identical to the one we buy. What we're really buying is a lie. In case the lie doesn't move us enough, the product we now have can be programed to deteriorate. Razor blades that dull quickly, stockings made to run, car bumpers designed to suffer damage at a 3 mph impact are a few indications of what is coming.

• And there are other deceptions. A most apparent case in point is the current flood of lottery-game gimmicks. We are not talking about whether the gambling is technically illegal or not, but rather about the question of deception within the game. There are pervasive and implicit deceptions in the simple failure to let the player know the approximate odds of winning the prizes. One game implies that because there are "three ways of winning" the odds are somehow enhanced. Or consider the prevalent practice of giving all the winning tickets to the first wave of players, then using their testimony of instant riches to promote a game that in reality has few, if any, large prizes left.

• During the first quarter of 1968 ten specific products (not corporations) spent over $30 million on TV advertising alone. Deceptions are widespread among those products most advertised on TV. For example, Salem, Winston, and Kool were among the top advertisers over this period, spending almost $10 million among them on

TV over three months, trying to convince millions of people that death-and-disease-dealing smoke is like fresh air, springtime, and cool mountain brooks. The current Newport ad repeats the word "refreshing" five times. Another three of the top ten for the first quarter of 1968 were analgesic companies, Anacin leading the pack with expenditures of over $4½ million. The ads for all three are blatantly and persistently deceptive: Anacin claims that two of its magical pills "contain as much of this [unnamed] pain reliever as four of the other [unnamed] extra-strength tablets," pointing out, of course, that one shouldn't take four of the other; Bayer advises that "Doctors and public health officials" recommend aspirin when flu strikes as one of three recuperative steps, and that since Bayer is pure aspirin . . .; Bufferin claims to go to work "in half the time."

We took our own look at the scientific and legal history behind these claims. We wanted to find out whether there were any significant differences in the speed with which competitive analgesic pills relieve pain, the degree of that relief and its duration, whether they relieve tension and depression, and whether they cause gastric upset. From a public health standpoint, the last point is the most important because there are strong indications that aspirin—the sole ingredient in some and the major ingredient in all of these preparations—can irritate the stomach lining so much that it causes internal bleeding, with possible serious consequences.

Four university studies of analgesics have been conducted—at the Johns Hopkins University, Boston University, the University of Oklahoma, and Dartmouth

College. The Johns Hopkins results showed all preparations about equal except that Anacin and Excedrin produced more gastrointestinal ill effects than Bayer, Bufferin, or St. Joseph's. This report was published in the *AMA Journal* of December 29, 1962, and Bayer seized upon the results for advertising purposes. The Dartmouth study found all products tested equally irritating to the stomach (Bayer, Anacin, Bufferin, B.C. Powder). At Boston University the conclusion was that aspirin and phenacetin, the two ingredients in almost all of the analgesics, had virtually no effect on tension. The Oklahoma study showed no difference in speed of relief among Anacin, Bayer, or Bufferin.

About the end of the fiscal year 1965 (July 30), a new form of analgesic—the time capsule—hit the market. Studies made by some of the manufacturers showed that its analgesic components were no better than ordinary products; it was marketed anyway.[1]

For thirty years Geritol has been permitted to lie blatantly to Americans, telling us that we should buy and take Geritol if we feel run-down or listless. The fact is that the number of people with these symptoms who would be helped by Geritol is almost infinitesimal. Yet these symptoms are indicative of a number of other afflictions, afflictions that should lead one immediately to a physician, not to a bottle of substantially useless Geritol.

• There are many other products relevant to health that are advertised in a manner that is questionable at the least. All of the mouthwashes, for another example, make

[1] Analgesics investigation led by Andrew Egendorf of the Harvard Law School.

claims about getting at the "cause" of bad breath and of "killing germs." They all claim to last "longer." But what the consumer is not told is that mouthwashes cannot totally destroy bad breath. Primarily, mouthwashes merely cover up the odor and leave the mouth with a burning sensation. This sensation is not the by-product of bad breath exculpation—it is the interaction of the excessive alcohol content of the products with the delicate tissues of the mouth. Many dentists have testified that the common mouthwash irritates the mucous membranes of the mouth. Medicine has yet to determine if this weakens the gums and causes teeth to be damaged sooner than they might otherwise. As in the case of cigarettes and other products, substantial statistical evidence will not establish the deleterious effects conclusively until the substance has been tested for a number of years. But one thing is sure: the ads will give no hint about the uncertainty of the product's effects. Listerine is even encouraging people to gargle several times a day to "prevent colds and flu." Not only will the mouthwash have an insignificant effect, if any, on preventing these ailments, but the very gargling with the substance three or four times a day when its long-run effects are in doubt is risky business. Even at best, it is useless. None of the commonly sold mouthwashes is recommended by the American Dental Association.

• This problem is similar to the "brightening toothpastes," which are highly abrasive. Their greatest danger is to those over 35, the age when many adults (approximately 25 per cent) begin to suffer a general gum recedence. This exposes part of the root or cementum above the gum. The highly abrasive material common to the "whitening toothpastes," while possibly dangerous to enamel itself, is more likely to be dangerous to ce-mentum. On January 1, 1969, the American Dental Association issued a warning about the product. How many Americans know of the warning? Probably no more than a few thousand. Yet the makers of Plus-White, Ultra-Brite, Ipana, Macleans, and others seem to feel no compunction about withholding this information. In-deed, they feel no compunction about continuing to advertise the sex appeal and general virtue of abrasive toothpastes.

• The makers of Cope, Vanquish, Dristan, aspirins, sprays, gums, drinks and syrups, pills and supplements, and all sorts of "combinations of ingredients" assure us that their products work magic on all varieties of ail-ments, real or anticipated. There is a marked resem-blance to the miraculous-elixir barkers of the nineteenth century. However, today's pitchmen pay $20,000 to make each commercial and several hundred thousand to pre-sent it, and they reel off their spiel to 30 to 60 million Americans at a crack. A 10-cent lie can pay for it all and more.

• Much the same problem is presented by butter and certain margarines, colas, many coloring agents and pre-servatives, and the false sweeteners of diet soft drinks. Preliminary research indicates that they may harm internal organs. There are no ads concerning the possible dangers or ill effects of the product to health. There is no information from the product advertisement itself and none from the supposed competitors. Can such omissions be regarded as anything but deception? And today such deceptions can be perpetrated upon more people in less time than ever in the history of man. Yet, the Federal government, through the Federal Trade Commission, is empowered by law to enforce the prohibition of all deceptive practices in interstate commerce.

• Tire ads are an example of misleading safety representations to the consumer's detriment. Firestone Tire, for instance, has been issuing campaigns that are filled with deceptive and inaccurate assertions. In two of these campaigns, Firestone made claims that its tires had "met or exceeded the new [Federal] tire testing requirements for some time" and later that its Wide Oval Tires "stop 25% quicker." Not only did Firestone refuse to substantiate these claims upon request, but their truth is also directly contradicted by numerous tests that show the Firestone tire to be among the most unsafe. They show it failing the Federal standards on many tests and indicate that the Wide Oval Tire has absolutely no greater braking capability than the standard tire. The details of these campaigns, the citations of contrary evidence, and the description of FTC collusion with Firestone are discussed later in "The Failures," pp. 35–95.

• Other ads flooding the TV networks that are deserving of inquiry at the least include the Shetland vacuum cleaner test, in which the machine's suction supposedly draws a resistant bowling ball up a plastic tube; the Ken-L Ration "butchers" who can't tell the difference between Ken-L Ration and real beef; the Colgate toothpaste claim that it is "unsurpassed," implying superiority; the assertions of Crest ads; the use of government tar statistics by Pall Mall; the Johnson Lemon Wax demonstration with unnoticeably disparate rags; the Cold Power claim to be "germproof"; the Bravo wax representation that detergents absolutely cannot dull the surface; that Mrs. Filbert's Diet Safe Margarine ad implying that if you can pull one inch of flesh off hubby's triceps he is too fat and will therefore die prematurely (unless saved by Mrs. Filbert's, of course); the Shell ads about "platformate"—which almost all gasolines contain; the "Persona electra-coated" blade; and on and on and on.

Why are some of these products not questioned, tested, and—if found dangerous or fraudulent—why are they not subject to the standards of truth demanded by law, morality, and common sense? Why can one sell a cigarette, whose truly distinguishing characteristic must be the production of disease and death (not to mention addiction) and fail to notice that fact? By what criteria is it not deception? Why is the basketball player Rick Barry, idol of millions of children, permitted to claim that Milky Way candy bars are "good food"—good for you because of the milk in the chocolate and caramel and the eggs in the nougat?

The Special Prey

While we talk about the stomachs and pocketbooks, supermarkets and television screens of all Americans, a particular crisis exists in the effects of these trends and practices on the lives of ghetto residents. Modern technology, especially in communications, has created rising expectations among the impoverished. Impatient for the material goods they are enticed to buy through radio and TV—that are apparently in plentitude all around them—they are particularly susceptible to the con man.

• First, they are prey to rampant fraud in credit arrangements. Daniel Jay Baum, writing in *The UCLA Law Review* in 1967, cites evidence from sociological studies of credit-buying in ghetto areas.[1] The findings indicate that one ghetto family in four has been victimized by time-payment plans. Frustration is the result in people who for the first time get a taste of the luxuries common to the rest of America, but who are required to pay substantially more for them and are then deprived of them by hidden accelerator clauses or delinquency provisions. The merchant retains the product for reconditioning and another sale. The ghetto resident must lose the comforts he has briefly enjoyed and is tempted to steal to stay even.

• But credit frauds barely scratch the surface of unfair and deceptive practices in America's ghettos. There are hundreds of flourishing rackets in our nation's poverty-stricken areas, all of them feeding on a desperate hope for improvement of self or neighborhood and almost all run by white, outside businessmen who exact enormous profits. Very few of these practices come to the attention of middle-class America, fewer still to the FTC. Most of them operate through appeals to the poor man's dreams. The victim is usually told that if he invests a certain

---

[1] "The Federal Trade Commission and the War on Poverty," 14 *The UCLA Law Review* 1071 (1967).

amount or buys an initial stock of goods, the investment will return with huge profits. Hard work might be involved (usually selling), but the attraction is provided by the short time he is told he will have to wait and by the flexible provisions for the initial investment (usually anything he has). Invariably, the victim is told about numerous people who have just made fortunes this way. Sales rackets of all kinds—pots and pans, magazines, encyclopedias, silver, fences, drink dispensers, insurance, and so on—deprive thousands of poor people of their life's savings.

Magazine sales, chinchilla rackets, and mail-order insurance work through straight, personal misrepresentation. A salesman will state that he must sell a certain number of magazines or face deportation to the country he arrived from. Or a consumer is assured that if he purchases several thousand dollars worth of chinchillas, he will be able to reproduce the investment into a veritable fortune without risk. The animals usually die, and sales are confined by agreement to the company selling the animals initially. Finally, the parent of a Vietnam soldier is likely to be solicited by insurance companies that strive to give the impression that they are forwarding a policy with the consent of the son and with the approval of the U.S. Army.

There is another type of fraud that victimizes the salesmen themselves as much as the consumer. The chinchilla swindles have this element as well as typical misrepresentations about the product, because the victim is considered part of the business. The most serious misrepresentations in this type of fraud are made to the salesmen, who are actually the ultimate consumers and the most viciously exploited victims. Usually, the product does not matter in these schemes; it is but a vehicle for the sale of a "chain-letter" type of promotion. For example, a person is invited to buy a drink dispenser in order to be a part of the "system." He is then given a hard-sell pitch through films, lectures, and so on about the riches he is bound to accrue. He is sold one of the oldest swindles known to man, yet in the unsophisticated ghettos of America, it works with devastating effectiveness. People are promised a proportion of the profits of the people they sign into the program (who must themselves buy dispensers, naturally) and a proportion of the profits that these people will gather from the people *they* sign into the program. At a $15-profit per unit, a mere ten sign-ups, if *they* each make a mere ten sign-ups, builds until riches seem imminent. The resemblance to the now-outlawed pyramid clubs is not accidental.

The encyclopedia misrepresentations are a prime example of a large-scale swindle that has elements of both direct misrepresentation to the consumer and misrepresentation to the salesman. This is also the area that has elicited the most vigorous FTC action. Unfortunately, that action consists of a dozen cease and desist orders that have had absolutely no visible effect on the practices. And these are not small, fly-by-night companies. The most reprehensible practices originate with the large companies: Britannica, Collier's, Field Enterprises (World Book), and Grolier's (Americana). Salesmen are promised minimum salaries ($500 per month "guaranteed" in the case of Encyclopaedia Britannica), which never materialize after work commences. Meanwhile, consumers have to put up with all sorts of harassing gimmicks about "trial sets" being "placed" in the home free—with bills appearing later. Salesmen are known to represent themselves as school officials who threaten expulsion of the child in school if sets are not purchased for "educational therapy." The longevity of some of these practices is attested to by the still-active FTC cease and desist order against Americana Encyclopedia to stop the "special-placing" routine. The practice is still a standard part of the Americana's pitch. The order was issued in 1949. The FTC has not taken action to enforce the order through court action, although it has the authority and indeed the responsibility to do so.

• A most lucrative variation of the sales racket theme has appeared in the home-improvement swindles of the past decade. Playing upon the strong desire of the ghetto resident to improve the appearance of his home and neighborhood, the exploiters sell aluminum siding and storm windows and doors that soon deteriorate. The contracts signed by the victim often contain confiscation clauses. Many residents lose their life's savings and their homes. The total take in this racket alone each year is well into the millions. Consider this beside the $55 million taken in robbery of all forms in 1968.

It would be an oversimplification to say that the enforcement of the law against criminals in business alone would have prevented the riots of recent years or that it would stop crime. On the other hand, there is little doubt that if law-and-order advocates had been enforcing the law against dishonest businessmen for the past decade, there would have been some limiting effect on crime born in the ghetto.

III

THE FAILURES

THERE IS A PIECE of heroic statuary in front of the Federal Trade Commission's building in Washington, D.C., that symbolizes the purpose of the agency as set forth in its founding statute. The statuary depicts an unruly and powerful horse—American business, a danger and a menace unharnessed—being restrained by a strong and determined young man, the FTC. But the FTC is neither young nor young-thinking, it is not strong nor does it seek to be strong, and it has no desire to restrain. Indeed, the Commission does not view American industry as a wild horse at all, but rather as a docile beast who now and then needs a mild "whoa."

The responsibilities given to the FTC demand that it see business as a sometimes unruly animal. That it does not is evident. Its Chairman,[1] Paul Rand Dixon, recently opened a typical address—to a business audience in North Carolina—with these words:

---

[1] The other Commissioners are Philip Elman, A. Everette MacIntyre, Mary Gardiner Jones, and James M. Nicholson.

I've come here with the high hope that I can persuade you that the Federal Trade Commission is not the social-istic, bureaucratic, damnyankee tool of the devil that may have been pictured to you. Instead, I'd like to convince you that you've got a friend in the FTC—a real friend . . .[1]

But the FTC cannot hope to be "a friend" to the busi-nessmen except by vigorous regulation. Under the pres-ent regime at the FTC, a businessman who suffers because of a competitor's unethical practices must either adopt the same practices or commit economic suicide. If he complains to the FTC, he must struggle to survive in virtuous poverty for years while the case is being litigated and while his competitors rake in their fortunes. Most American businessmen are no more suicidal, pure, con-cerned, or foolish than the FTC is a young, strong force restraining the economy for the public welfare.

The attitude of the Commission represented by its Chairman's remarks was spawned through business and political connections and arrangements, and it pervades every aspect of FTC activity. A cursory examination of FTC public relations reveals one outstanding feature of the Commission's operation—its continual and consistent violation of its own statute with regard to deceptive prac-tices. The FTC itself is one of the most serious and blatant perpetrators of deceptive advertising in America. It has avoided Congressional or other investigation or review for a decade by responding to the vector theory of power—feeding and serving those who would or do

---

[1] "Needed: A Combined Attack," address before joint meeting of the Better Business Bureau and Advertising Club, Winston-Salem, North Carolina, January 8, 1968.

threaten it. Substantially, this means feeding and serving big business and Congressional interests.

We will show how the FTC has failed to do its job in four specific regards. Unless it addresses itself to correcting these failures, the FTC will never work with any effectiveness:

1. The FTC has failed to detect violations systematically.

2. The FTC has failed to establish efficient priorities for its enforcement energy.

3. The FTC has failed to enforce the powers it has with energy and speed.

4. The FTC has failed to seek sufficient statutory authority to make its work effective.

See No Evil: The Failure to Detect Violations

According to its own testimony, the FTC's primary means for detecting deceptive practices is, indeed, to wait for the virtuous businessman to inform on his wicked competitor. Most businessmen, however, find it easier and more profitable to join in the deceit than to complain to the FTC. The second source of initiation the FTC relies upon is "mailbag notice"—that is, complaints from consumers (which the FTC calls "applications for complaint").

These complaints from the public do not provide notice of many problems. First, the FTC is not going * receive complaints from a person who is not seriously injured. A consumer will not be motivated to complain about petty frauds (even if on a massive scale) since the FTC has no refund power, and no private civil suit can be based on an FTC order. The FTC is not going to receive complaints from those who cannot trace the difficulty to a particular product, say mouthwashes. The FTC is not going to receive complaints from those who do not know of other alternatives. Because of product fixing and product complexity, the consumer often doesn't even know he is being deceived, or he probably perceives the historic futility of appealing to the FTC.

Another fallacy in the mailbag approach can be found in America's ghetto problems. Here, as finally shown by the Commission's own study of consumer deception in Washington, D.C. (begun in 1965 at the insistence of Senator Warren Magnuson of Washington), the situation contradicts the Commission's assumptions about deceptive practices. Ghetto victims do not care about the flood of inferior goods—they are numb through the lack of any higher expectation. If they wished to complain they would not know how. They don't have lawyers, and they don't know a thing about the FTC.

The mailbag source of complaints is certainly useful, relevant, and can often be indicative of certain types of outright fraud. In the case of chinchilla advertising, for example, which deceptively promised huge profits with little work for raising chinchillas at home, it was the pitiful letters, such as the following, from people who had seen their life's savings disappear before their eyes that first alerted the Commission to the problem.

Watervliet, N.Y.
April 5, 1968

Attorney Seidman
% Federal Trade Commission
30 Church St.
New York, N.Y.

Dear Mr. Seidman:

Information and purchase of my chinchillas was from the telecast by Division West shown on WAST, channel 13. Their representative assured me with 1 males and seven females that I could easily earn up to $6,000 a year; their offspring producing well, right in my cellar. Transactions took place April 6, 1966. After two years of hard work on my part I have received $26 from my investment. With no end of red tape, commissions, etc. too numerous to mention.

Never did they mention fur chewing which laboratory testing from many parts of the world have yet to find any reason. The only solution was they must be destroyed. No medicine or knowledge at Midland Laboratory has aided after many months of testing. Fur chewing, disease and breeding problems is a great loss to chinchilla ranches. All information plainly shows it is impossible to bring in monetary returns to even pay for feed in these circumstances.

Division West stated in the purchase contract of April 1966 that they would prime, pelt and market our animals. The above promise is a serious one as without that service the rancher does not have the facilities or the know how for priming, especially as it requires refrigeration as no persons home can be kept at a temperature of 38–40°.

Pelting service of that kind would be $3.95 each by the corporation. October 1967 notices were sent out stating that they could no longer prime the animals as they had no facilities with large and numerous buildings they claim they have. The Central Avenue branch opened for 2 years, just long enough to help the salesmen. All ranchers were left high and dry without a supply depot. Another fact is that the rancher has no way of knowing the value of the pelts. We were told the market price for pelts was $17 to $40. On 8 pelts I have received a return of only $26. The price of the string was $2145.00.

Sincerely,

But this source is not sufficient. The FTC must establish vast new means of detection. It must initiate aggressive and intensive investigations, particularly in ghetto areas. It must monitor TV and radio carefully in a general surveillance effort. It must, perhaps, establish FTC investigative teams in every trouble spot, particularly in the ghettos. It must, perhaps, require presubmission of certain categories of advertising.[1]

At present, the FTC monitors haphazardly and occasionally, accounting for no more than 10 per cent of investigation targets. Several sources have confided that the Commission's one TV monitoring operation, which consisted of several matrons watching the set, was discontinued because they "paid too much attention to

---

[1] According to *Advertising Alert* No. 2, February 12, 1962, the FTC monitored 50,000 scripts from TV and radio presubmissions. Investigation has revealed this claim to be doubtful at best. Even if true, such monitoring would do little toward detection of visual deceptions; nor do experts prescreen copy.

the programs" (mostly soap operas) and would leave for snacks during commercials. It is obvious that there must be alert and extensive monitoring operations with pre-screening by expert engineers, doctors, and other professionals.

It is also obvious that the FTC's single ghetto investigation, which was rather forced down its throat, was not a sufficient approach to ghetto victimization. The aluminum-siding scandals, the magazine sale and cookery rackets, the myriads of get-rich-quick schemes that prey with particular viciousness on the poor will not be discovered through talks before trade associations, Washington hearings, or mailbag complaints. Distributorship and sales rackets with alleged pyramiding returns, magazine classified sections filled with lucrative traps, and the continuous barrage of false claims and enticements will not be ended without truly aggressive FTC action.

First Things Last: The Failure to Establish Priorities

An analysis of FTC cases other than those involving textiles, furs, and country of origin reveals a curious geographical distribution. Out of all of these cases—reported in the *FTC News Summary* from July, 1964, to July, 1968—there resulted 248 cease and desist orders. Thirty of those orders—12 per cent of the national total—were issued against businesses within Washington, D.C., and its immediate environs. Most of those were in the suburbs, only a few relevant to the capital's ghettos.[1] If FTC activity reflected the distribution of population, Washington and its vicinity would have to include over 24,000,000 people to justify this concentration. The fact that Washington is so treated is a reflection of two things. First is the inadequacy of detection measures beyond Washington. There, at least, the staff members at the central office are asked to monitor deceptive practices themselves as they watch TV at home. Second is the response to personal problems of Congressmen living in the District or its suburbs.

Ideally, priorities must be carefully set to help those who need help most. Deceptions and other practices that endanger health and physical safety must come first. Practices affecting the poor must be given high priority because the poor can afford to lose less. The number of persons affected must also be weighed. For that reason, unconscionable practices by large corporations that sell products across the country must get urgent attention.

While conducting one of the first studies of the FTC as far back as 1924, Gerard C. Henderson found a priority system lacking: "the Commission is handling too many cases, and it should exercise a greater discretion in selecting those cases which involve questions of public importance." [2] There has never been any argument that the FTC should ignore small cases, if it can get funds to handle them. But Congress limits the Commission's re-

---

[1] The FTC does have plenary jurisdiction within Washington itself, but this does not extend to suburban Virginia or Maryland. Further, those cases in the District are within FTC jurisdiction because they generally involve interstate commerce.

[2] Henderson, *The Federal Trade Commission*, p. 337.

sources—the FTC has at no time made vigorous efforts to expand its funds. It should deal with the more important issues. Fearful of big corporations, declining in activity, ineffective in enforcement, the FTC basically allocates its dwindling energies to the prosecution of the most trivial cases. Precedence depends on the origin of the application for complaint. If the source is a favored Congressman, some action is assured. Otherwise, it is up to chance or a personal contact with the agency.

Twenty-five years after the Henderson report, the Task Force of the Hoover Commission made its report. The situation was unchanged:

As the years have progressed, the Commission has become immersed in a multitude of petty problems. . . . The Commission has largely become a passive judicial agency, waiting for cases to come up on the docket. . . . In the selection of cases for its formal dockets, the Commission has long been guilty of prosecuting trivial and technical offenses and of failing to confine these dockets to cases of public importance.[1]

More recently, Professor Carl Auerbach conducted an intensive study of the FTC on behalf of the Administrative Conference of the United States. He, too, observed that "the important question is whether the Commission has a system of priorities by which it is guided in discharging all the tasks entrusted to it by Congress. To date, the answer is no." [2]

---

[1] *Hoover Commission Report,* 1949, pp. 125, 128.

[2] Auerbach, "The Federal Trade Commission," *Minnesota Law Review,* 48, 1965.

And, according to the statistics and all available evidence, the answer is still no. Just recently (1968), the Commission reconsidered for the third time a case that had occupied over four years of Commission and staff time in which the main issue was whether or not a watchband chain representing less than 1 per cent of the value of the finished watchband should be explicitly labeled as originating in a foreign country or not. They eventually decided that it should.

A recent and typical reflection of FTC priority failure is found in the 1968 Senate hearings on appropriations. For some five years the Commission has been mentioning imminent studies of the food-market situation. Meanwhile the problem has become more and more critical. Several reports were compiled, none of which seemed to have had any effect. Senator Gale McGee of Wyoming suggested the necessity for a continuous examination of the food industry so that concrete and effective action might be taken to correct dangerous practices. Testified Chairman Dixon before the Senate Subcommittee on Independent Offices:

> I agree with you, the Federal Trade Commission was created by Congress to carry on this type of study, but this is something that if we are to carry on, the necessary money should be supplied. For you to say, well, why do you not do it out of what you have—you are going to give us a terrible management problem. At the present time we are receiving some 9,000 complaints per year and we have not as yet dared to say to anyone, "We are not going to look at your matter, because it is not as important as some of the rest." We are having difficulty in handling our increasing workload with our available staff.

I hope you will restore the $225,000 and that you do not overlook our new program to do something about nearly $400 million worth of wool imports into this land.

Mr. Dixon's statement makes clear the low priority he gives an investigation into a multibillion-dollar industry of critical importance to every man, woman, and child in the country. In the same breath he is obviously much interested in pushing the politically fruitful issue of wool imports.

The FTC preoccupation with textile and fur laws reflects a continual theme in FTC enforcement policies: the great importance attached to anything involving the protection of American business interests. Certainly, many of the FTC's legitimate activities, at least theoretically, benefit honest businessmen as well as consumers. But these laws are an ideal "out" for the Commission. They can spend great energy on their enforcement, offending mostly the Japanese and other foreign producers, while spending relatively little effort policing deceptive practices or restraints of trade by American big-business interests.

The FTC pretense is that Congress specifically requested enforcement of the textile and fur laws. Of course, this is true, but Congress has also given the FTC a mandate to prohibit deceptive practices and restraint of trade. Even so, the pretense is irrelevant because it is the FTC, not Congress, that must allocate FTC resources to carry out its legal mandate according to sensible criteria.

Within that sanctified textile and fur category the FTC has set priorities with disregard for the consumer's welfare. By the Commission's own figures, over the last five years an average of under 15 per cent of the cases handled by the Bureau of Textiles and Furs have dealt with flammable fabrics. The flammable-fabric cases should represent a high-priority category for enforcement because the protection of life is involved. Such figures could, of course, reflect merely a smaller number of violators in the flammable-fabrics area, but there are other indications that the FTC has ignored flammable-fabric enforcement activity. First, there is the small number of civil penalties—involving a maximum of $5,000 a day for violation of a cease and desist order—invoked against flammable-fabric violators, despite the potential danger involved. Although the Flammable Fabrics Act was passed in 1953, the first civil penalty action was not brought until 1966, and there have been altogether only three civil penalty actions in the field. In addition, our interviews and conversations with staff and Commission members reveal a lack of concern or a lack of awareness about the need for a higher priority for flammable-fabric enforcement as against wool, fur, or textile.

A more explicit example of myopia in this sphere, involving collusion and secrecy, is a recent episode concerning a shipment of flammable Japanese rayon. Chairman Dixon cited the assurance of voluntary compliance obtained with regard to this shipment as an example of the advantages of "persuasion" and industry "guidance" before the 1965 House Appropriations Hearings. And, indeed, the FTC had barred future shipments of the dangerous materials into the country. But the Chairman failed to mention that most of the shipment had already been distributed to clothes manufacturers, and that the staff had strongly recommended to the Commission that the rayon then in the hands of the manufacturers be seized. In fact, the enforcement order or agreement that the Chairman boasted of represented a gross and mysterious concession to the defense attorney, Peyton Ford, a powerful member of Washington's corporate law establishment. Not only is this episode indicative of a lack of concern in a matter affecting the health and safety of the American consumer, but it is also an example of the lengths the Chairman will go to to protect interests dear to him and of the brashness with which he will cloak his activities. That rayon is right now on the backs of American men, women, and children who are unaware that it is dangerously flammable.

The D.C. Study

The FTC claims priority planning for the benefit of "those most in need." Yet its efforts since 1965 in its District of Columbia project have been so small and half-hearted that it could be called a paper program for publicity purposes. Here is an example of what we call "scoping"—choosing one case for action from a number of a related kind. The D.C. project opened 98 investigations over a period of three years. From these, 27 formal complaints were issued; then only 19 final orders were entered. Of the final orders only 7 were accepted as adequate. The others are still "under investigation." [1]

---

[1] *FTC Report on District of Columbia Consumer Protection Program,* 1968, p. 1.

The D.C. project is also an outstanding example of the reluctance of the FTC to use rigorous enforcement penalties—its right to penalize up to $5,000 a day for each violation of its final order. Moreover, according to the D.C. report,

> Of the 15 final orders for which compliance orders have become due, seven reports of compliance have been accepted by the Commission. Four respondents did not submit any compliance reports and three respondents submitted inadequate reports. All seven cases were accordingly sent into the field for investigation . . . the Commission has put itself in a position whereby it can state unequivocally . . . that if violations are going on they are known to the Commission and are under active investigation.[1]

However, despite the Commission's knowledge of these violations, it has still failed to recommend a single penalty. If the Commission's resources are so limited that it cannot afford to divert more funds to the vital D.C. project, it might at least consider making more effective use of the legal resources it does have.

Even in this critical area of ghetto deceptive practices, the Commission has relied upon the weak tool of voluntary compliance to stop offenders. On January 25, 1969, the Commission dismissed its charges of deceptive practices against the D. C. ghetto store Marlo's Furniture World. In its decision, the FTC ruled that Marlo's "placed deceptive classified ads in newspapers, made

---

[1] *Ibid.*, p. 12.

misrepresentations concerning cash deposits, inaccurately described the nature of its products and failed to inform customers that sales contracts involving credit might be re-financed with lending institutions." The basis for the dismissal was the company's verbal promise to mend its ways. This was too much for even the normally conservative Commissioner A. Everette MacIntyre. The Commissioner wrote a vigorous dissent, charging that the action was a "misuse of the Commission's informal procedures." He stressed that Marlo's practices had been found to be "wilfully misleading and indeed verging on fraud."

One major point stressed by the Kerner Commission Report on Civil Disorders was that the ghetto poor justifiably felt that they had been unfairly exploited by local white merchants.[1] This exploitation was also documented by a 1968 report prepared by the FTC's Bureau of Economics.

Senator Magnuson states the plight of the poor consumer most movingly:

> Entrapped by devious clauses in contracts and duped by the lies of fast-talking salesmen, many of the victimized poor do not have the faintest notion of what has happened to them; they know only that they have been badgered by bill collectors, lost their jobs, seen their furniture or homes swept away, and that the law is somehow implicated.

---

[1] *Report of the National Advisory Commission on Civil Disorders,* chapter 8, section III, "Exploitation of Disadvantaged Consumers by Retail Merchants." See also *The Dark Side of the Marketplace,* by Senator Warren Magnuson, and *The Poor Pay More,* by David Caplovitz.

Worst of all, these poor people are nearly helpless to fight back, for they do not know their rights nor how to exercise them.[1]

In the American tradition of despairing debtors, which dates back to Shay's Rebellion in 1787, the ghetto dwellers used violence to attack the source of their frustrations. Thus, during the D.C. riots in 1968 there were selective firebombings of local merchants and finance companies.

Washington was not singled out for such treatment. As Senator Magnuson wrote:

> A number of witnesses called before the Governor's Committee investigating the Watts riots did testify that . . . the prime targets of violence . . . were the establishments of merchants who engaged in sharp selling practices. . . . During the catastrophic Detroit riots in June, 1967, arsonists . . . systematically burned stores known to engage in sharp selling and credit practices.[2]

Filling the Time

Aside from the wool and textile concentration and the great watchband chain identification case, there are many examples of FTC passivity. For, while the Commission either ignores or delays requisite enforcement activity against Geritol, analgesics, Firestone, the home-improvement frauds, auto warranties, medical devices, the ads mentioned in the first section, and the like, it has

---

[1] *The Dark Side of the Marketplace*, p. 53.
[2] *Ibid.*, p. 57.

spent great sums of manpower and money on items such as the following, extracted from the *FTC News Summary:*

The Federal Trade Commission has ordered Korber Hats Inc., Fall River, Mass., to stop using the word "Milan" to describe the material of men's straw hats not manufactured in Italy of wheat straw. (July 3, 1964)

Ogus, Rabinovich & Ogus, Inc., 304 E. 45th St., New York City, has consented to an order forbidding it to falsely invoice and advertise fur products. . . .

The Commission's complaint charges that the concern has omitted and abbreviated required information on invoices covering various fur products. (January 26, 1966)

The Federal Trade Commission has issued its consent order forbidding Alex Kirschner, a paint and varnish brush manufacturer trading as Kirschner Brush Co., at 58 W. 15th St., New York City. . . .

The Complaint charges that, contrary to these representations:

1. The brushing part of the brushes marked "Pure Chinese Bristle" is not made entirely of hog bristle imported from China, but is in fact composed of a mixture of bristle and some other material; and,

2. The brushing part of the brushes marked "All Pure Bristle" is not made entirely of hog bristle. . . . (February 8, 1968)

These examples are not extreme but typical of FTC enforcement activity. They were selected almost at random from the total of consent and cease and desist orders issued between July 3, 1964, and June, 1968. In Section 2 of the Appendix we have charted these orders, dividing them into one category for textile and fur cases (excluding flammable fabrics) and country-of-origin misrepresentations and another for all other deceptive practices. Although the "all other" category is not the least devoid of trivia, it is the textile category that monopolizes matters relatively unimportant to the American consumer.

The "all other deceptive practices" category contains less than half the total orders issued over this four-year period. When we subtract from its dismissals the selling of re-used golf balls and oil, the use of fake prizes to entice people, and the mislabeling of soldering irons, we have only 188 cases left from the 562 formal enforcement actions. Of these 188 remaining cases, 30, or almost one-sixth, are from the Washington, D.C., area. Most of the 158 cases for the rest of the country fall into about half a dozen categories of important (although very specific) deceptive practices—involving home-improvement schemes, collection agencies, chinchilla ranches, and insurance. One is the rather primitive bait and switch tactic, in which a merchant—generally small—jacks up the enticingly low prices he has advertised as a come-on.

But even the statistics for the areas important to the consumer are illusory. The most important category, for example, is probably the home-improvement frauds, particularly aluminum sidings.[1] But the twenty or so cases treated by impotent enforcement procedures have not

---

[1] According to a letter (November 28, 1967) from Chairman Dixon to Senator Magnuson, "An official of a large lending institution has estimated that there are over 50,000 firms engaged in the sale and installation of residential siding and storm windows."

even scratched the surface. These frauds are so wide-spread [1] and so severe in their effects that people (usually the poor) are virtually robbed of everything they own. Often their house is taken, their wages garnisheed. Some have committed suicide as a result. The effect of the racket on the victim is similar to the impact of the chinchilla frauds, but it is much more extensive and the abuses are particularly aggravated throughout America's ghettos. Further, the situation has been getting progressively worse. The Commission's response, aside from the five or six scattered and toothless orders [2] issued each year as a gesture, is contained in the Chairman's response to Senator Warren Magnuson's appeal for action:

> Due to major manpower commitments to the packaging and cigarette programs, the District of Columbia Consumer Protection Project, the automobile warranty and softwood lumber inquiries, bait and switch practices in the sale of frozen food and other promotions, the insurance investigation, and many other efforts reflecting a high degree of public interest, I can give you no assurance that additional personnel can be assigned to attack this swelling workload promptly.

Bait and switch practices in the sale of frozen foods? Chairman Dixon amplified his attitude in his response

---

[1] Commissioner Mary Gardiner Jones, in her "Non-Agenda Matter Re: Home Improvement Cases," February 8, 1967, indicated that "The Consumer Council's Report lists home-improvement fraud as one of the biggest areas of consumer deception today."

[2] In his letter of November 28, 1967, to Senator Magnuson, Chairman Dixon said "The home improvement situation is one of these in which the ultimate enjoining of fraudulent practices is not an adequate deterrent to the unethical operator."

both to the problem and to the suggestions by Commissioner Jones and others that the FTC intensify its enforcement powers for cases involving personal fraud. In the same letter, he wrote to Senator Magnuson:

> One important factor, constantly on my mind, is that while much of our effort is in the interest of the consumer, the great majority of honest, reliable home contractors in the country are equally deserving of this protection.

The Commission gives much lip service to the final consideration in a rational priority system, the size of the company involved in the transgression. Yet in actual fact the FTC does very little when violations involve large companies—unless those violations are extremely trivial.

For example, according to the attorney in charge of prosecuting home-improvement frauds at the FTC, large finance houses and the large aluminum companies, such as Alcoa and Reynolds, encourage the fly-by-night operators who directly defraud the poor. Producers have not only supplied the distributors and swindlers with inferior products, but made credit-plan suggestions and helped in advertising and promotional setups. Yet nothing substantial has been done to threaten these powerful interests and their Congressional lobbies.

The many examples of deceptive ads or at least marginal ads we discussed in the "Crisis" section come primarily from large companies. A cursory examination of FTC actions reveals the extent of the Commission's fear of or friendship with big business.

Section 3 of the Appendix analyzes the size of all companies on the FTC docket for the first quarter of 1968 on

the basis of sales. Twenty-nine of the thirty-three
panies involved are so small that they are not listed
any major financial directory, which means that their
total *assets* are below $500 thousand. Only one company
had sales of over $500 million.

The FTC's reluctance to go after big companies often
lies in its fear of their vast and brilliant legal staffs—
particularly if formal action is called for. But there are
also cases of outright pressure from corporate or legal
contacts, often exercised through the Congress.

In a letter dated October 25, 1968, to John Schulz, one
of the members of our project, Chairman Dixon could
not answer a question asking for the size on the basis of
annual sales of all deceptive-practice respondents. He
explained:

> Annual sales are not maintained as general information in
> deceptive practice matters. This is simply because sales
> volume is frequently only one of many considerations in
> assessing the impact of a particular practice.

In other words, since this is only one of several elements,
it is not computed at all.

Don't Rock the Boat: The Failure to Enforce

The Federal Trade Commission has found several,
separate methods for not performing its enforcement
duties properly under existing law. First, the FTC has
allowed a general decline of formal enforcement activity
of any kind. Instead, it has shifted—unwisely—toward

"voluntary" enforcement tools. To compound that, it has also permitted compliance by those whose practices have been challenged to become almost entirely voluntary. Finally, the FTC saps all of its enforcement programs by excessive delays.

The Decline

The decline in formal FTC enforcement goes back to the early 1960's. Since then, formal enforcement has declined not only in relation to the Gross National Product, the growth of the advertising industry, and the rise in complaints received, but in absolute numbers as well. Except for a brief resurgence in 1967, the number of complaints issued by the Commission has been steadily declining since 1963 (see Appendix, Section 4).

The FTC has also shown its passivity—in the face of increasing consumer, ghetto, and advertising problems—in the decline of investigations. Fewer and fewer investigations have been completed since 1964 (see Appendix, Section 5).

Finally, the FTC shows its passivity by an increasing tendency toward what we have described as "scoping" in its enforcement—choosing one case for action from a number of a related kind. (In this regard, the FTC has been somewhat less rigorous than the Ancient Mariner, who "stoppeth one of three.") The applications for complaint in deceptive practices alone are in the thousands (6,399 in 1966, with the annual figure now approaching 9,000). Yet investigations cover only one in every eight or nine applications for complaint (see Appendix, Section 6). And this is after the crank letters have been thrown out and applications have been screened for relevance and appropriate jurisdiction. Omitting Congressional applications, which are rarely ignored, the ratio for response to applications from the public becomes even lower. After 10 per cent or so of the complaints are investigated, not even one in ten of the *investigations* results in a cease and desist order. (Section 7 of the Appendix shows that decline.) One out of four, however, does result in an assurance of voluntary compliance—a boy scout's oath not to practice the deception in the same way again. (See Appendix, Section 8.) All together then, about one in 35 applications for complaint results in an assurance of voluntary compliance, and approximately one out of every 125 results in formal action of any sort.

The numbers in these charts are not in themselves a conclusive condemnation. It is only when viewed with the rising need for action, the lack of a priority system, and the other failures we discuss that the FTC reveals its betrayal of the public interest.

The 1965 Civil Service Report's evaluation of the FTC workload backs up our own impressions and findings:

The traditional measure at the Federal Trade Commission has been casework expressed in such terms as numbers of 7 digit investigations initiated (this is a code identification of cases designated for formal investigation), complaints issued, and cases docketed for litigation. *By all of these measures caseload has been declining. Several managers expressed the fear of running out of work* [our italics]. . . .

With the changing mission orientation since 1960 there has been a decline in formal cases from 1,931 that year to 1,421 in fiscal year 1964. During this same period, the number of cases docketed for litigation also decreased: from 503 to 49. (Using the same years, employment increased from approximately 700 to 1,150.)

Despite these caseload and employment trends, the agency expresses itself in dire need of more employees while giving repeated assurances that the employees in the enforcement bureaus are fully occupied, if not with casework, with providing advice and counsel within the framework of the "new approach." Beyond these assurances of management we must also consider the following, in concert with the workload data above, in making a judgment as to whether the Federal Trade Commission has enough, or perhaps too many employees to accomplish its mission:

1. On the basis of widespread comments *there appears to be less than full utilization of Hearing Examiners*
2. *High officials spoke openly of the rapidly approaching time when there would be no more casework to occupy the staff*
3. *Trial Attorneys, as a reflection of this, expressed concern that they would soon be out of work*
4. *It has been suggested, in consideration of the above, to abolish the Bureau of Industry Guidance.* This suggestion is perhaps motivated by the apparent paradox that this Bureau was established to provide the kind of advice to industry that the Federal Trade Commission claims is accounting for that part of the time of the staff in the enforcement bureaus not devoted to cases.[1]

---

[1] *Civil Service Commission Report*, 1965, p. 26.

Since 1965, when this critical report was issued, the situation has deteriorated even more (see the FTC's own statistics in Appendix 4). The FTC ignored all of the suggestions of the Civil Service Commission. Hearing examiners are still not fully used, caseload has declined even further, and the Bureau of Industry Guidance has not been abolished.

The Shift

The general decline in formal enforcement at the FTC has been accompanied by greater reliance on "voluntary" enforcement tools. The FTC rationalizes this as the most efficient means of enforcing the law. Nothing could be further from the truth.

The Commission can do more than slap the hand of a violator of the law. If a deception concerns a misrepresentation about food, drugs, flammable fabrics, or furs, it can recommend criminal action to the Justice Department. Otherwise, the FTC has available the clumsy but *potentially* effective cease and desist procedure. Here it can issue a complaint against a transgressor and, after a hearing and appeals, can establish an order to cease and desist from the unfair or deceptive practices. This order itself carries no punishment—but if it is violated the agency can recommend civil actions to the Justice Department (limited to damages of $5,000 a day by law). Yet the Commission's major individual enforcement vehicle is the assurance of voluntary compliance. A businessman who gives an assurance merely promises, not even under oath, that he will not repeat the specific deceptive practice challenged by the Commission. A repetition generally brings about another assurance.

The FTC also has so-called industry-wide approaches —guides and trade-regulation rules. These are generally responses to inquiries from businessmen who want to know how far they can go without breaking the law. The guides themselves, however, do not have the force of law. They can be effective if a group of competing businessmen of high ideals all agree to refrain from a particular deceptive practice. Unfortunately, a businessman without high ideals has an incentive to deceive consumers even when—perhaps especially when—his competitors are dealing honestly.

The voluntary methods of enforcement permit commercial wolves to take not just one "free bite" (as is the case even with cease and desist orders since they also do not inflict penalties for past offenses) but two or three.

As actually administered, voluntary enforcement is even more inadequate than it seems. Trade-regulation rules and assurances are often poorly drafted, the rules sometimes too broad (no more than restatements of the statutes they are supposed to elucidate), the assurances too narrow (forbidding only a *specific* deceptive activity, ignoring other likely tactics). The advisory opinions that business calls upon the FTC for are frequently given with inadequate background information. And, like trade-regulation rules, they tend to be mere paraphrases of vague statutory language.

The Commission's methods of checking compliance with guides, rules, assurances, and advisory opinions are abysmal. The FTC checks by requiring compliance reports, which it does not verify. Compliance with guides and trade-regulation rules is policed by industry-wide compliance surveys conducted by the small staff of the FTC's Bureau of Industry Guidance. But these surveys tend to be interminable, and nothing is done about individual violators until a survey is completed.

For example, the Commission issued tire-advertising and labeling guides, effective as of July, 1967. Ever since, a broad survey has been in progress on the advertising claims of some 200 tire brands, according to Thomas Egan, the FTC staffman handling it. Mr. Egan said, "no efforts to secure compliance with these guides will be made until the survey is complete," and he would not venture a guess about that distant date. The matter came up in regard to our questions about the recent Firestone ad which proclaimed that Wide Oval Tires stop "25% quicker." Apparently, incomplete comparisons ("quicker" than what?) are a clear violation of Section 5(b) of the FTC's Tire Advertising Guides. The section states: "Dangling comparatives should not be used."

The FTC's inadequate handling even of voluntary enforcement suggests that the policy was adopted largely to mollify growing consumer indignation without having to punish the guilty.

Even Chairman Dixon realizes that voluntary enforcement will not work unless backed up by some strict, binding enforcement techniques. In the 1967 Senate Appropriations Hearings, he stated:

Now the follow-through comes. If most accept this [rule or guide], but if one, two or three or four [or . . . ?] do

not, we must get tough here, because there is no reason to
expect the majority to stay in line long if others do not
comply.

The problem is that the Commission does not get
tough with those who don't stay in line. The Commission
maintains that a major reason for voluntary enforcement
is to allow a businessman erring through ignorance to
clean his own house. But the FTC takes exactly the same
posture toward a businessman who has trespassed with
open eyes in his own interest. It is like giving equal
traffic fines to a driver who inadvertently fails to see a 20
mph speed-limit sign and exceeds the limit and a drag-
ster who knowingly and recklessly violates the same law.

Rather than vigorously use its enforcement tools, the
agency has declined to act with energy or speed. It has
refused to recommend criminal action and has sought to
give the violator of the law not just the one free bite provided by the cease and desist order procedure but many
more. The additional bites are provided by the FTC's
refusal to bring action against those violators who ignore
and even flout established cease and desist orders and by
the invention of the complex system of "voluntary" enforcement procedures. Rather than bite down hard on
the violators, the agency prefers a toothless attempt to
gum them to death.

When the FTC does issue a cease and desist order not
only is there not enough checking of compliance, but
even what little there is has great defects. The FTC
checks how its cease and desist orders have been obeyed
by requiring violators of the law to file "compliance re-

ports" within sixty days, in which they are to tell the
FTC that they have abandoned their objectionable practices and taken effective steps against recurrence. Again,
the FTC does not independently verify the accuracy of
these reports and can neither threaten nor impose a
penalty for false reports. (Imagine, if you will, a judge
writing a convicted bank robber, whom he has freed
without sentence: "Dear Sir, please let me know if you
have stopped robbing banks.")

With so much room for evasion, it would seem that
very few violators could be caught in noncompliance.
That any are is a tribute to the Commission's laxity even
in the face of outright defiance. Section 9 of the Appendix shows how few penalties the FTC exacts. The sums
are relatively small—for corporations—and there has been
a strong trend over the last two years to get after textile
and fur violators only.

This record yields its meaning all too clearly in the
light of a candid interview with Barry W. Stanley, chief
of the FTC's Division of Compliance in its Bureau of
Deceptive Practices. Mr. Stanley stated that the FTC
detected "hundreds of violations each year," resulting in
cease and desist orders. The detections usually come
through complaints from the public or competitors, but
the violations, he said, were dealt with "informally."
Informal handling means approximately, "Go and sin no
more"—giving the commercial wolf yet *another* free bite,
even after he has been ordered to cease and desist.

The most blatant current example is the much-publi-
cized Geritol case. In 1967, after years of "investigation"
and litigation, the FTC ordered the J. B. Williams Com-

pany, the manufacturer of Geritol, to stop misrepresenting the product as a generally effective remedy for fatigue. In spite of this order, later affirmed by the Court of Appeals, Geritol's TV advertisements have changed little in emphasis, as most viewers well know. In an unusual departure from normal procedure—based possibly on impatience with the lethargy of the compliance-division staff, the Commission itself recently held "a public hearing to hear oral argument to determine whether TV commercials for Geritol violate its order to 'cease and desist.' " [1] After the hearings, the Commission issued its finding that since the order Geritol commercials have

> not only failed to comply with the order, but . . . are no less objectionable than the commercials denounced by the Commission when it issued its original order herein.[2]

Having discovered a clear violation of an outstanding cease and desist order, did the Commission announce that it would seek "civil penalties" against Geritol's makers? No, it merely warned them to stop "flouting" the order and to file by January 31, 1969, a report showing what steps were being taken to tone down the commercials; and in case that report is inadequate, the Commission threatened to take steps to assure that its orders "do not continue to be flouted by respondents."

The compliance report issued by Geritol contained transcripts of the company's most recent ad campaigns. They seemed to be specifically aimed at providing unob-

---

[1] FTC News Release, October 29, 1968.

[2] FTC News Release, December 13, 1968.

THE FAILURES

jectionable material for the report. The new ads did not in the same way refer to "tiredness" and openly admitted that Geritol would help only a small minority of people who felt run-down. The FTC staff found the company not yet complying. The new commercials still contained substantial misrepresentations. Yet, the Commission did nothing. Meanwhile, Geritol, having performed for the compliance report, has since gone back to the more extreme and blatant deceptions—tying tiredness, the medical profession, and health to a product that has very little connection with any of them. One may well ask what lesson other companies condemned under FTC orders will learn from the highly visible Geritol case.

The staff chief in charge of compliance with cease and desist orders leaves no doubt that his enforcement philosophy is seriously misguided. In our interview, Mr. Stanley indicated that he believes cease and desist orders are merely administrative directives and that violations are not a serious matter in themselves. All that has to be done is to seek future compliance by gentle persuasion. In this manner, the FTC took nine years to issue a cease and desist order to Collier's Encyclopedia for "lengthy and blatant use of deception" in selling its product by implying that the encyclopedia was given free to buyers of the annual supplement.[1] How many more sets will be sold this way before the FTC takes another slow and ineffective step to halt the practice?

It is a strange philosophy. Cease and desist orders represent authoritative judgments by the Commission, and often on appeal by the courts, that a particular prac-

---

[1] See *New York Times*, February 27, 1969, p. 19.

tice constitutes a violation of law. As such, they must be viewed as binding prohibitions against repeating the same sorts of conduct. To permit respondents to play fast and loose with such orders is to dissipate whatever authority and integrity the Commission possesses as a governmental agency.

More important, cease and desist orders at present represent the FTC's most potent general enforcement weapon. If it is to be at all effective, however, respondents and potential respondents must believe that the FTC will deal severely with violations. The permissive philosophy and practices of the compliance staff make the Commission's enforcement program a portrait of impotence. Or, viewed in a more sinister light, it is powerlessness with a purpose.

The picture is even worse for the strongest weapons the FTC possesses in the important areas of food and drug products and flammable fabrics. Here, besides the civil penalties of damages up to $5,000 a day, the Commission is empowered to bring criminal action against offenders. In fiscal 1967, it brought no criminal cases. In fiscal 1966, it brought one, involving the fur act. In 1965, none.

The FTC also almost never seeks preliminary injunctions, although it has power to do so under all textile and fur acts, as well as the food and drug provisions of the FTC Act.

Section 5(c) of that act gives the Commission an additional power similar to preliminary injunction. The law allows the FTC to declare a halt to challenged activities when a respondent seeks court reviews of cease and desist orders, pending judicial review. To our knowledge, the Commission has not invoked this power for years. We found that the philosophy of Mr. Stanley is not unique. Our interviews with other division and bureau chiefs revealed that it permeates the top echelons of the Bureaus of Deceptive Practices, Industry Guidance, and Textiles and Furs. This poses a serious threat to reform within the agency.

Even more serious, this philosophy is shared by a majority of the Commissioners themselves, as indicated in their interview statements, and in innumerable speeches, especially those of Chairman Dixon. It is apparent also in an exchange between the majority and Commissioner Philip Elman over his recommendation that the Commission make a legislative proposal to the 90th Congress to centralize the prosecution of consumer fraud in a single Federal agency—not the FTC.

Mr. Elman had been concerned because a particular fraud might simultaneously be susceptible to prosecution by the Justice Department, to administrative proceedings by the FTC, to action by the Post Office, etc. The majority, in purported response, engaged in a general discussion of the relative effectiveness of criminal penalties and the Commission's industry-wide and "voluntary" approaches as enforcement tools. In that discussion, the following amazing statement appears:

> One of the great advantages of the FTC's administrative responsibilities to protect the consumer is that the Commission is not limited to action involving "prosecution for consumer frauds" as Commissioner Elman proposes. The needs of consumers go far beyond protection from fraud.

Thus the Commission has power to investigate, hold public hearings, issue guides, prepare informational material and take other informal measures to solve a problem confronting consumers. These powers are far more efficacious than the single power to prosecute after the problem has taken its toll of consumers even though this power is also an essential element of law enforcement.

This statement contains a tangled mass of misstatements, distortions and half-truths, all of which cannot be discussed here. What can and must be commented on is the Commission majority's belief that such efforts as issuing industry guides protect consumers more effectively than criminal penalties.

This is simply not true. Properly viewed, the problem is general deterrence—keeping businessmen from perpetrating their first act of fraud. In discussing general deterrence, it is irrelevant to focus on those who have already broken the law. A regulator's major concern must be to hold the line against those who have not yet broken the law. The Commission thus misses the point in criticizing criminal prosecutions for taking place *after* someone has broken the law. Rather, it should focus on the effect such a prosecution will have in keeping other potential violators in line.

As an illustration, assume that businessman A (for, say, Anacin) violates the FTC Act. Now, let us imagine that the FTC does its job, and he is prosecuted and convicted of consumer deception (under an as-yet unwritten amendment to the Act). Or, alternately, the FTC acts as it usually does and tells him to stop, requiring him only to write a letter saying "I've stopped and won't do it again" (an assurance of voluntary compliance). Now, compare the likely impact of these two ways of treating A on businessmen B, C, and D (Bufferin, Cope, Dristan?), who may be considering an increase in consumer deception themselves. There is little doubt that the first enforcement method will be more effective in keeping the maximum number of businessmen in line.

It thus seems clear that since tough enforcement is much more efficient than mild, voluntary methods, it is highly irresponsible of the Commission to neglect the tough in favor of the mild—while complaining of inadequate resources. This is especially true since all criminal prosecutions sought by the FTC would actually be carried out by the Justice Department, using that department's resources.

In addition, that statement of the Commission majority seems to imply that FTC voluntary enforcement methods, unlike criminal prosecutions, can stop deceptive practices before they can harm consumers.

The Delays

One inside observer has called the Federal Trade Commission a "real fantasyland." Proof is plentiful. Two recent deceptive-advertising cases, involving companies called Ronnie, Inc., and Doughboy Industries, were closed because the papers had been lost. "Despite diligent search," read the memorandum to the Commission for each case, "the file in this matter cannot be located."

The case of the Crawford Corporation, which involved interlocking directorates in the prefabricated housing industry, was dropped on April 4, 1969, when it was discovered that the defendant had withdrawn from the prefabricated housing business in the early months of 1964—*five* years earlier.

These cases are extreme examples of poor staff work, but they also illustrate what can result from time lags. And delay, unfortunately, is a way of life at the Commission, built into even the smoothest-run deceptive-practices case. One typical case provides an illustration. On April 4, 1962, the FTC field office in Chicago began to investigate the Vollrath Company of Sheboygan, Wisconsin, for "making false savings claims and misrepresenting the construction, efficacy, and other features of stainless steel cookware it sells." Among other things the the company advertised that its "Vacumatic cookware would prevent certain diseases and satisfy hunger with less food because of the retention of vitamins and mineral content." *Four years* later, on July 20, 1966, the case was given to the Bureau of Deceptive Practices for prosecution. Yet another year passed before a hearing examiner made the initial decision in the case, and still another year before the Commission made its final decision.

In this case the time lapse from investigation to final decision was six years. The average time lapse is four years, with two years of investigation in the field and two years of prosecution in the central office. And there are measures available for a company whose practices have been challenged to delay action even longer. Some have stretched litigation out over 20 years and more.[1] Until the end of that average four years, the company can flout the FTC. There is no punitive power until after the order has been established, and very few transgressors take the Commission's enforcement power seriously until actual sanctions are imminent.

Even where deceptive practices are of long standing or companies are too small to oppose the Commission legally, there are other delays. After the cease and desist order is issued, compliance must be checked. A failure to comply at this point should result in a civil suit by the Justice Department. But here, too, there are delays. And, although a company must file reports within sixty days, many cases in FTC docket files indicate that often a year or more elapses between the effective date of a cease and desist order and acceptance of a "satisfactory" compliance report. In a substantial number, no compliance report is apparently ever filed.

In one case violations of an outstanding cease and desist order were uncovered and documented in detail, but a move to prosecute for civil penalties was delayed for so long that the necessary evidence was invalidated by statute of limitations. The case involved a large food company in the Midwest which deceptively advertised freezer and food plans. The consumer was promised substantial savings in food purchases if he bought a large freezer from the food company. After buying the

---

[1] Section 5(c) of the FTC Act gives the agency the power to petition for an order to take effect *immediately* pending further long drawn-out court appeals. To our knowledge it has made no use of this power in recent years.

freezer, however, he would discover to his dismay that he had to pay regular retail prices. The FTC opened its investigation in 1959 and a final cease and desist order was approved by the Commission in October, 1962. Two years later in September, 1964, the Commission received a compliance report. On October 13, a month after the compliance report had been received, a contradicting complaint was registered with the Commission. The ensuing investigation took a year and a half to complete, and, yet, when the evidence was forwarded to the compliance division of the Bureau of Deceptive Practices, the attorney in charge decided personally to adopt a "wait and see approach." Twenty-eight months later the case was forwarded to the Commissioners with a recommendation not to seek civil penalties because of obscure "evidentiary weaknesses" and the attorney's opinion that the defendants were "very respectable individuals who would not likely violate the order." This reasoning did not satisfy the Commissioners, who sent the case to the General Counsel's Office for comment. On April 3, 1969, the General Counsel reported back to the Commission that indeed the evidence was excellent, but unfortunately, because it had been collected more than five years earlier, it was barred from court by statute of limitations. Thus seven years after discovering a major deceptive practice the FTC could only confirm the fact that, despite their outstanding order, the consumer was still being fleeced.

One of the Commission's indirect enforcement weapons is the power to inquire and investigate. Congress has granted the Commission broader investigatory powers

(Section 6(b) of the FTC Act) than any other regulatory agency. But here, again, delay minimizes power. The reasons are less likely to be sloth, inefficiency, or bad law than direct business collusion, with delay serving to cloak an issue in secrecy and to avoid action on it. The excuse that a problem is "under study" for years and years allows the Commission to keep it from public scrutiny under the Freedom of Information Act,[1] while giving the impression that something is being done or will shortly be done.

The Commission's behavior with regard to automobile advertising, drugs, auto warranties, food and gasoline games, tires, medical devices, and many other problem areas can be traced to purposeful delay aimed at protecting certain interests. A study into a given area is announced with fanfare and expression of concern, and a target date is set. As time passes, the due date is quietly extended and extended again.

An investigation of the deceptive claims of analgesic companies began over a decade ago. The disposition of investigations resulted, primarily, in four dismissed complaints after years of tests and years of still continuing deceptive ads.[2]

The deliberate suppression of the report on auto warranties is another example of delay for political purposes. The report was initiated in 1965 and was released in late 1968 only because Ralph Nader had then obtained a copy

[1] The Freedom of Information Act, which was passed on July 4, 1966, makes allowance for withholding some confidential material. See below pp. 111, 115–16.

[2] See *FTC News Summaries*, April 13, 1965, July 7, 1967, and November 30, 1967.

and prereleased it. No one can or would dispute that a report should not be divulged to everyone until it has been completed. But the FTC first submitted the report, confidentially, to industry interests so that they could check the accuracy of certain data without giving the same opportunity to consumer groups (for instance, the Consumer's Union, publisher of *Consumer Reports*). The Commission then delayed release although the report was in final form. The real reason for the proposed plan for suppression lay in the contents of the report, which was highly critical of GM, Ford and Chrysler. Whether release would have eventually occurred is academic now, but there is little doubt based upon our interviews that Chairman Dixon was determined to suppress the report at least until after the election to avoid alienating Henry Ford II and other business interests who were contributing heavily to Hubert Humphrey's campaign.

Since releasing the report, the FTC has settled down to conduct lengthy hearings and consultations with the automobile companies for the ostensible purpose of producing a trade-regulation rule. Again, the most important factor in this process is that no real action will be taken in the foreseeable future to correct flagrant violations of auto warranties. That the public is still being abused during these long delays has been made painfully obvious to the members of the project, who, since the issuance of our report, have received hundreds of letters on the subject. A random example was written by the owner of a 1968 Chevy Caprice:

In the warranty book, page 5, it states that plugs and the air filter are covered for 2 years or 24,000 miles whichever comes first. Up to the present time there has been two sets of plugs put in and the filter replaced but to our expense. Why would they write it up in the warranty and not stand behind it? At the present time there is 21,015 miles on the car.

In case after case the sad story is repeated—malfunctions supposedly covered by warranties are repaired at the owner's expense or are poorly repaired by dealers who are not adequately reimbursed by the automobile companies for warranty work. We have received many letters from aggrieved consumers who are forced to return to the dealers time and again for repair of the same flaw. One consumer had his brakes lock six consecutive times shortly after supposed dealer repairs under the warranty. He and many others in the same situation had the dangerous condition corrected only by going to an independent garage where, of course, payment is necessary. Despite their knowledge of these abuses and their power to stop them, the FTC continues to delay any meaningful action.

The singularly unusual case of the FTC's action on deceptive cigarette advertising is indicative of what the FTC would be capable of if properly directed and motivated. As a knowledgeable inside critic of the FTC noted, "The job the FTC did in the case of cigarettes is a classic example of solid administrative work. It represents what the agency should be doing in many other fields."

In June of 1962 because of prodding from the FTC for guidance on the issue of cigarettes and health, the Surgeon General started his now famous study of the health effects of cigarettes. His report was issued on January 11, 1964, and on January 18 the FTC gave notice of a rule-making procedure for cigarette advertising. The notice was only *pro forma*, however, since the FTC had already pulled together a task force a month before the completion of the report. By June, 1964, the rules that provided for a strong health warning on *all* cigarette advertising were promulgated. The powerful cigarette lobby had to make exceptional efforts to get special legislation passed to restrict the FTC's rules to the present mild warning on cigarette packages and cartons. That law, however, will have expired in June, 1969, which, barring renewal, would free the FTC to enforce its 1964 rules. So the FTC *can* be effective, if it acts quickly and decisively, ignoring the various industrial lobbies.

But the highway-automobile lobby is too strong for the weak-willed FTC. This group, which has foisted miles of needless concrete on the nation at the expense of much-needed mass transportation, consists of automobile manufacturers, highway contractors, and subsidiary industries including tire producers. Just as the auto corporations have influenced the FTC on warranties, so have the tire manufacturers prevailed upon the FTC not to regulate their advertising in the face of blatant deceptions. The delay and secret manipulations to avoid interfering with Firestone's deceptive advertising are revealed in an exchange of letters among Firestone, Inc.,

Chairman Dixon, and Ralph Nader concerning two specific ad campaigns.

The first ad campaign by Firestone began in the fourth quarter of 1967. It was composed of massive circulation media advertisements headlined: "Raymond C. Firestone Talks About the Safe Tire." The copy went on to say that "on November 10, 1967, the Federal Department of Transportation issued a new set of tire safety standards. Firestone tires already meet or exceed these new tire testing requirements and they have for some time. . . . All Firestone tires have met or exceeded the new testing requirements for years."

In a letter dated January 1, 1968, Mr. Nader asked Mr. Firestone for substantiation of this statement. The letter went unanswered. As the advertisement appeared first in most major news magazines in late 1967, the FTC could not have missed it. In case its surveillance was wanting, Mr. Nader notified Chairman Dixon in a letter of February 13, 1968, and requested that the Commission obtain substantiating data from Firestone. Mr. Nader argued that any company soliciting a customer's trust with such safety claims ought to be ready to back them up, especially when it purports to surpass a specific government standard of safety. Refusal to produce documentation makes such an ad presumptively deceptive. In reply, on February 19, the FTC, in the person of Chairman Dixon, asked the writer for information showing the ad to be deceptive, instead of using its unique legal powers to obtain substantiation directly from Firestone. Again, the Commission was passive when asked to confront a large corporation. Chairman Dixon did say that the Commission had opened an investigational file, but not an inquiry under Section 6(b); the question of an inquiry, Mr. Dixon added in a letter of March 26, could not be decided "until an investigation is completed." An investigational file is automatically opened on receiving a letter of complaint—a classification that permits all such materials to be confidential under the FTC's interpretation of the Freedom of Information Act. The Commission displayed a total lack of interest in several facts: Senator Gaylord Nelson has in his hands a large number of complaints about Firestone's Wide Oval Tires; Firestone tires had failed tests conducted by Electrical Testing Laboratories for the National Bureau of Standards in January, 1966; and the safety-testing program of the National Highway Safety Bureau showed each of eight Firestone tires failing in at least one of the Federal government's safety standards. Although knowing of these developments, the FTC did not even make an inquiry of any of these sources.

The second Firestone advertising campaign of deception also began in 1967 and continues to the present time. The ad touts the Wide Oval Tire by saying that it "grips better. Starts faster. Corners easier. Runs cooler. Stops 25% quicker." This is a deceptive advertising practice *per se* according to Section 5(b) of the FTC's own Tire Advertising Guides, which expressly forbid dangling comparatives, as we have seen.

No investigation is necessary; no substantial allocation of time or funds is required. These ads comprise a national campaign on the part of a very large tire manufacturer via the mass media. The deception is serious, simple, and clearly communicated to millions of readers and is effective in inducing purchases of the tire offered. The Commission, however, did nothing.

On August 6, 1968, Ralph Nader wrote Chairman Dixon urging the FTC to act against this deceptive advertising. On August 15, 1968, Chairman Dixon replied that the matter "is receiving consideration." He added: "You may be assured that such action as may be found warranted by the facts will be taken in the public interest." On September 20, 1968, Mr. Nader wrote to Chairman Dixon, notifying him that a Ford Motor Company representative had told the National Highway Safety Bureau that "The braking capability of the Wide Oval Tire is no greater than that of the standard tire." Despite years of investigations and industry guides, stretching back to 1936 and extending up to 1966, the Chairman's response to a literal and specified violation was to refer to yet another investigation, thereby excusing the concealment of Firestone's answer to a legitimate citizen inquiry.

It is common to discover that a still-pending investigation was used five or six years previously to justify inaction then. For instance, consider the food and gas-station gimmick games. They are commonly deceptive in several respects, and restraint of trade is often involved as well. Pressure has been building up recently, and in a memo of February 20, 1968, Rufus Wilson, chief of the Division of General Trade Restraints, found it necessary to make the standard promises about another investigation of promotional games in the food and oil industries. By late December, 1968, as reported in *Advertising Age*, it appeared that a staff report on the subject was finally made public—a member of the press having secured a copy and reported on it. *Advertising Age* indicated that the Commission was also finally considering promulgating a trade-regulation rule covering these games. This means it will hold additional hearings, delaying regulation for another substantial period of time. But this is not unique. Back in 1963 Joseph Shea, Secretary of the Commission, wrote with regard to File No. 643 7007:

> By letter to William J. Jeffrey, President, Merchandising Marketeers, dated November 15, 1963, the Commission granted an advisory opinion concerning a retail food promotion scheme.

> This is to advise that that advisory opinion is rescinded. This course is required in the public interest because the subject matter of that advisory opinion is currently under investigation by the Commission.

The Federal Trade Commission has always considered lottery-type inducements, particularly when deception was involved, violations of the deceptive-practice laws. In a memorandum of October 11, 1967, Michael J. Vitale, chief of the Division of General Practices of the Bureau of Deceptive Practices wrote:

> the element of consideration need not be present in order for a scheme to be illegal. . . . The Commission found it sufficient to establish the illegality of the scheme, that [the participant's] return would vary greatly with his willingness to take a chance.

If the scheme is illegal even when the participant does not pay directly for a chance, why does the Commission still fail to initiate continuous, rather than sporadic, investigations? Perhaps the answer lies in the size of the companies involved in these deceptions. They include the Texas Company, Esso Oil, and large supermarket chains.

An investigation was opened in 1963. When pressure continued to mount from complaining consumers after that 1963 effort faded into an empty void, another investigation was begun in 1966 to fill the gap. In 1967 the Bureau of Economics requested and received authority to use subpoena power under Section 6(b) to gather information on the game operations. In March, 1968, after all that investigation, the bureau issued a *preliminary* report, which nevertheless contained enough information to bring immediate action against a dozen game operators. For, although almost all the games seem to be deceptive, some are patently deceptive—even disregarding the question of gambling's legality. The big promotion "Let's Go to the Races" is typical of these. This is from a consumer's letter in the March, 1968, report of the Bureau of Economics, still unreleased:

. . . [This game] is broadcast over television through all States and in our opinion is a rigged and deception scheme in which the main factor of success exclusively depends upon creation of atmosphere of a false illusion . . . "Let's Go to the Races" were filmed long time ago in Sunshine Race Track in Florida (which is not even now in existence). . . . Public is unaware also that on tickets which they are getting, the winning horses were already prearranged by the promoters with a chance to win five dollars being about 2,000 to 1.

Our own investigations substantiate the information in this letter. The report contains hundreds of complaining letters that outline blatant and fraudulent deceptions in nearly every part of the country.

A final note is that Congress has helped the Commission to investigate this problem—Representative John D. Dingell of Michigan has held hearings on the use of gasoline promotional games.[1] Again according to *Advertising Age*, the agency's possible forthcoming staff report bases most of its discussion of these games (not including grocery-store promotions) not on its own data but on Representative Dingell's hearings.

The story behind the FTC report issued in 1968 on the misgrading of softwood lumber also points up typical delays. The problems of misgrading included not only deceptive markings on lumber products which seriously affect the structural quality of frame houses, but also the balance of power in the marketplace between large and small lumber companies. The Commission admits in its introduction:

The question of possible misgrading of softwood lumber has confronted the Commission almost continuously since July of 1962. On March 13–15, 1967, a hearing was held on the subject before the full Commission.

---

[1] House Small Business Committee, Subcommittee on Regulatory and Enforcement Agencies, June 20, 1968–July 11, 1968.

This report details some administrative history. It reveals the profound and endless paper shuffling that precedes even the most elementary reports:

See File No. 632 3104, opened July 24, 1962. This matter led to the establishment of a general file, File No. 652 3319 captioned "Lumber Grading Agencies and Distributors, Unnamed," investigations under which resulted in the establishment of two additional files (File Nos. 662 3151 and 662 3154). On October 12, 1966, the Commission approved a proposal by the Bureaus of Industry Guidance and Deceptive Practices to hold a hearing . . .

Although so much time has elapsed since the deceptive grading of softwood lumber was brought to the Commission's attention, the Commission has yet to act. The report, issued on May 6, 1968, recommended the promulgation of a trade-regulation rule. In the light of past experience it will take at least a year if not more for the FTC to promulgate these rules. In the meantime other government agencies and Congressional Committees which might take action are restrained from so doing.

A classic case of FTC delay, publicized only recently through the efforts of Ralph Nader, involves the unauthorized Volkswagen dealers who have been selling used VW's as new. This practice has been going on for nearly a decade. Highly sophisticated reconditioning garages in West Germany prepare used Volkswagens—some of which have been involved in serious crashes and most having already clocked thousands of miles—for shipment to the United States, where unauthorized dealers resell them for new. The techniques of deception involved are readjusted odometers, price labels resembling new car labels, and false explanations, about, for example, rust observed by customers in which the damage is ascribed to salt-water contact during overseas shipment. Invariably, the year of the vehicle's production is changed (i.e., a 1968 model is redated to 1969), a practice facilitated by the VW's unchanging appearance from year to year. After the sale is completed, the defrauded motorists experience "rapid" deterioration of parts and sudden breakdowns. In some cases serious accidents have resulted from the failures of the used VW's to respond properly on the highways.

These facts have been documented in detail by two FTC staff investigations, one of which was closed in 1964 by Michael J. Vitale. In the other, legal action was overruled by William W. Rogal, then chief of the Commission's Washington field office and now an assistant bureau chief of the Bureau of Deceptive Practices. The Commissioners who reviewed the investigations were not given the complete files, but instead relied on the upper staff's interpretation of them.

Volkswagen America, Inc., has known of these practices for years, but has not made the problem public for fear of adversely affecting the sales of their new Volkswagens.

The extensive delays in the Volkswagen case resemble those in the "investigations" of tires, games, and softwood lumber. Those, however, involve the Commission's so-called "voluntary" and "industry-wide" enforcement tools (advisory opinions, industry guides, and trade-regulation rules). Here is clear indication that these methods of handling violations are not much more effective than the traditional "formal" approach by cease and desist orders. In fact, they may be worse, since cease and desist orders at least make asserted violations public.

"The Best We Can": The Failure to Seek Effective Resources and Authority

During the last decade, the Federal Trade Commission has done too little too late to give its enforcement some muscle. It has made little effort to seek adequate funds or manpower or statutory authority.

The Commission needs to multiply its staff and budget many times if it is to enforce its consumer-protection statutes. An agency that devotes perhaps half of its 1,200 staff members and annual budget of a little more than $14,000,000 to consumer protection cannot hope to police adequately the merchandising activities of hundreds of thousands of businesses. Home-improvement frauds alone provide a striking illustration of this. Charles A. Sweeney, who was until his recent death program review officer at the FTC, said in an interview that these frauds are so widespread that to stop them the FTC would have to spend an amount equal to its *entire* deceptive-practices budget.

The very magnitude of consumer problems is suggested by figures for mail fraud in this country. During the last fiscal year the Post Office received 150,000 complaints from consumers about incidents of mail fraud, up 11 per cent from the previous year. Postal inspectors made 1,082 arrests during this period, up 52 per cent over the previous year, of which 681 were convicted from previous arrests. This record stands in stark contrast to that of the FTC's, whose jurisdiction includes mail promotions as well as promotions through many other kinds of media.

The FTC's record cannot impress Congress, which could give it additional powers. Nor has the FTC performed in such a way as to justify a further investment. Too much is likely to be wasted in misplaced priority determinations, and in ineffective enforcement procedures. On its own side, the FTC has failed to crusade directly with the requisite imagination and vigor for expanded authority and appropriations. Appropriations hearings over the decade reveal that the Commission is quite content to let itself slowly wither into meaningless pontifications, with an occasional grandstand play.

In 1965, Chairman Dixon analyzed the agency's requests for budget increases as follows:

> This calls for an increase of $1,055,250 over the 1964 appropriations, but more than 80% of this increase will be required by costs over which our agency has only limited control—including $250,000 for a half-year cost of the January 5, 1964 pay raise . . .[1]

He was saying that, although the FTC was requesting new funds, they would not be applied to expanded enforcement.

Likewise, the Commission's request for 27 new personnel that year did not imply imminent general expan-

---

[1] 1965 Senate Appropriations Hearings, p. 388.

sion of consumer protection—since 25 of the 27 were for the relatively unimportant Bureau of Textiles and Furs.

When Senator Warren Magnuson asked Chairman Dixon whether he could get along in the other bureaus without additional manpower, the Chairman replied:

> Well, we would be in the same position we are in on antitrust, and our workload increases, and we know all we can do is promise we will do the best we can.[1]

The Chairman's passive attitude is consistent. In the 1967 hearings he stated heroically that

> Although fiscal 1967 is certain to confront the Federal Trade Commission with the heaviest workload in its history, the Commission is determined to tackle it with no increase in staff. . . . Not only are we not asking for additional personnel but we will be required to absorb $80,000 for mandatory within-grade promotions.[2]

And in 1968, more than one-third of the agency's requested budget increases was for 26 new employees to carry out new enforcement duties under the Fair Packaging Act, meaning no addition to important existing programs.

It is also necessary to take into account an additional factor when measuring the significance of the FTC requests. A large increase in personnel, say 6 per cent or so every year, would just keep the FTC even relative to the

---

[1] *Ibid.*, p. 415.
[2] 1967 Senate Appropriations Hearings, p. 474.

Gross National Product, which for our purposes here supplies a rough guide to the size and activity level of the business establishment the Commission is supposed to oversee. Actual increases do not even match this low standard, as the chart in the Appendix, Section 10, illustrates.

Even more important than manpower and funds is the expanded statutory power necessary to run a proper enforcement program. Two basic additional enforcement powers seem to be needed—the power to seek criminal penalties for certain violations and the power to seek preliminary injunctions in appropriate cases. Criminal penalties are necessary for compelling widespread compliance with the FTC's consumer-protection statutes. The threat of criminal penalties multiplies the efficiency of an enforcement agency by what is known in criminal-law theory as general deterrence. The more limited an enforcement agency's resources are, the stronger the argument for criminal penalties, since they produce maximum general deterrence; that is, they are the most effective in inducing the greatest number of potential law violators to behave. This is especially true of highly rational entities like corporations.

It is particularly important to apply criminal sanctions to dishonest corporate behavior, for it is far more damaging in contemporary America than all the depredations of street crime. Law and order must not stop at the doorstep of these massive and influential institutions.

The fact is, however, that the Commission has failed to press Congress vigorously for broader powers to seek the imposition of criminal penalties for violations of the deceptive-practices language of the FTC Act. In fact, the Chairman has recently gone on record specifically as *opposing* such powers, according to testimony given on a Senate consumer-deception bill sponsored by Senator Magnuson.

The Commission also requires the power to seek preliminary injunctions—which would allow the FTC to halt a challenged activity immediately, not only before a court appeal but before the delay of three to five years that comes in the FTC's own processing of a case. Preliminary injunctions are the only means of protecting the interests of the consuming public promptly. They could be reserved for cases in which violations of the FTC Act are relatively blatant.

Preliminary-injunction power would also put an end to much of the delay the FTC gets bogged down in. If a lucrative challenged practice is enjoined, a respondent gains nothing by wasting Commission resources in drawn-out litigation.

The FTC's history contains little effort to expand preliminary-injunction powers. Its legislative proposals (published in the agency's annual reports) include no reference at all to such powers in 1961, or 1962, 1963, 1964, 1965, or 1966. The 1961, 1962, and 1963 reports do include a half-hearted proposal to enact a law giving the Commission power to issue temporary cease and desist orders pending agency proceedings. Even this proposal is lacking in the next three years' reports. Consider the following statement about the 1962 proposal made by the Chairman in the 1963 Senate Appropriations Hearings:

You recall the President endorsed this piece of legislation, not once but twice. . . . It is controversial, sir. I think any time any agency or any arm of the Government is cloaked with any kind of temporay injunction powers, it should only be used in the most extraordinary circumstances . . .

Only in 1967, with the winds of consumerism blowing hard and with goading by the Senate Commerce Committee, did the Commission propose legislation that would provide power to seek temporary injunctions against any act or practice unfair or deceptive to *consumers*. But Senator Magnuson, not the FTC, was the moving force behind this legislation.

The FTC consistently plays a weak role in pressing for legislation. The inadequacy of the Commission's legislative record is reflected in the small number of legislative proposals it has made in recent years.

During Chairman Dixon's term in office, since 1961, there have been a total of thirty legislative proposals. Because of repetitions of the same proposal there have been only nine different proposals concerned with deceptive practices. Of these nine, only two have won passage. One placed blankets within the provisions of the Flammable Fabrics Act—an inclusion originally opposed by the agency because of its industry contacts. The other lent support to the Truth in Lending Bill. Of the remaining seven, four have been totally or partially repudiated by Chairman Dixon's policies and recommendations. These include temporary restraining-order power, preliminary-injunction power, and criminal-sanction power. The remaining three legislative proposals are relatively unimportant or academic or have not been pushed with even token vigor by the agency. These include the expansion of FTC jurisdiction over insurance and a "cooling off period" for door-to-door sales.

Meanwhile, the Commission ignores or takes no stand on recurrent, pressing problems. Thus, in 1967, the Commission refused to follow its own Commissioner Elman, who would have recommended legislation to deal with problems of drug brands and prices, product warranties, consumer representation, and hazardous household products. The Commissioners had several reasons for refusing to adopt Commissioner Elman's suggestions. But one in particular is characteristic—the claim that much more time was needed to investigate these problems thoroughly. In its statement on legislative proposals, the Commissioners said of Mr. Elman's suggestions, first, on drug legislation:

> The Commission is aware that the problems of drug pricing are currently under consideration by Congress. . . . The Commission has not had any opportunity to study the question. . . . The Commission cannot at this time reasonably propose to Congress the adoption of legislation on the subjects . . . without accompanying such proposals with careful memorandum analyzing in depth the need for such measures. . . .

And on statutory product warranties:

> The Commission has not included a proposal for legislation on the question of statutory warranties since it is of the view that a specific legislative proposal cannot and should not be put forward until the feasibility of such a

[93]

statute has been thoroughly considered, . . . The Commission does not have the kind of precise information as to the dimension [sic] of the problem which it needs in order to propose solutions, legislative or otherwise.

In these two cases the Commission's excuses are more transparent than usual, for the Commission *has* been studying just these questions. It has acknowledged in appropriations hearings that it has had various problems of the drug industry under investigation—at the insistence of Congress—since as early as 1960. As for automobile warranties (by far the most important of all warranty problems), the Commission has been carrying on an investigation since 1965, according to the 1965 *FTC News Summary*. It has, in fact, recently issued a 250-page staff report on the subject. While more "precise information" *may* be needed, the Commission's position seems disingenuous.

On hazardous household products:

On May 31, 1967, the Commission . . . directed its staff to undertake an investigation of electric shock hazards in household electric appliances . . .

On October 3, 1967, the Commission . . . directed the staff to complete its overall investigation . . . and to report its recommendations to the Commission.

It would be irresponsible for the Commission, therefore, at this time to make any recommendations. . . .

. . . The Commission['s] . . . own studies have not yet been completed.

Here, the Commission, writing in mid-1968, is obviously right to say that it cannot propose legislation. But it must take responsibility for the dilatoriness of its staff in completing important investigations on dangerous electric shocks. This sort of rationalization for Commission inaction—which is frequent—is particularly objectionable. It constitutes an attempt to rationalize failures to act by *earlier* failures—sort of pulling yourself down by your own shirttail.

The list of failures has been long. Some excuses will be legitimate, but the ultimate criticism has nothing to do with numbers—of budget allocations, of actions, of days for processing. The failure of the FTC has been its utter lack of effectiveness. It is this that must be understood, and unmasked so that it may be corrected.

IV

THE MASK

Like an aged courtesan ravaged by the pox, the FTC paints heavily the face it presents to the public. Because the failures go deep the paint that covers them has to be laid on thick— thick as a mask.

Keeping the mask painted on is perhaps the one activity the Commission dedicates itself to with energy. Its working materials are public relations, secrecy, and collusion.

Public Relations

THE FTC'S PUBLIC RELATIONS activities make for an image that is false and misleading. It abounds with false claims about effective detection, gross deceptions about priority policies, and misleading statistics about effective enforcement. These are borne through various channels, including the numerous speeches made by the Chairman, his testimony at appropriation hearings before Congress (and his related budget justifications), and special reports.

The standard devices include declaring all potential problem areas "under study" for years, taking action against a few easy and visible targets in a given problem area, making overly optimistic estimates or "projections" of work to be accomplished in the future, the creation and removal of differing categories of statistical analysis as the need to touch up the mask requires, and the failure, with certain exceptions, to face facts which might call attention to what is happening in ghetto America or in the advertising offices of corporate giants.

The annual reports provide examples as good as any. They outline a glib little world which simply does not exist, discussing certain (generally unimportant) problems which are implied to be the only ones extant, and listing the countermeasures taken to deal with them. They are filled with illustrations, such as a picture of the Better Business Bureau of Orange County, California (1967 Report, p. 69), or a chart from the *Pit and Quarry Handbook*, showing "Capacity Concentration in the Portland Cement Industry, 1950 and 1964" (1966 Report, p. 49). The 1967 Annual Report devoted 25 pages to a list of past investigations (mainly pre-World War II), but only four pages to consumer deception.

The annual reports, and indeed virtually all FTC public relations efforts murmur such noble phrases as:

> In selecting matters for attention, a high priority is accorded those matters which relate to the basic necessities of life, and to situations in which the impact of false and misleading advertising, or other unfair and deceptive practices, falls with cruelest impact upon those least able to survive the consequences—the elderly and the poor.[1]

And we are assured by the Chairman's testimony in the hearings of the Senate Subcommittee of Independent Offices for 1967 that

---

[1] 1967 FTC Annual Report, p. 17.

with our limited staff I can say to you that we are paying more attention to perhaps the 200 largest corporations in America that control in our basic economy a substantial share of the sales in the various industries.

Another misrepresentation involves the FTC compliance monitoring program for advertisements. In a 1962 Advertising Alert (No. 2, Feb. 12, 1962), the FTC stated that

> The review of written continuities [scripts] is supplemented by some direct monitoring of broadcasts . . . Attorneys determine whether the Commission Orders to Cease and Desist, and Stipulations, are being violated. Other commercials are analyzed to determine the effectiveness of Trade Practice Rules and the Guides program.

In a typical speech—before the Division of Food, Drug and Cosmetic Law of the American Bar Association on August 10, 1966—Chairman Dixon outlined a simplistic picture of the theoretical advantages of the FTC's voluntary enforcement measures. He categorically stated that "the Federal Trade Commission has faced up to the realities of its law enforcement job to an extent unprecedented in its 51 years of existence." The Chairman cannot be unconscious of his irony. The voluntary measures have failed entirely because of a number of fallacious calculations, and formal enforcement measures are declining in number, as we have seen. In addition, the Commission has made more specific claims. It has even pretended unblushingly to a quick dispatch of cases.

Another favorite misrepresentation of Mr. Dixon involves consumer-protection groups and interests. He relishes describing them as wild-eyed zealots threatening the values of federalism and free enterprise. Meanwhile, he sees himself as the chief bulwark against their conspiracy for government control and tyranny.

After listening to one of Mr. Dixon's speeches to a trade association, Sidney Margolius, author, columnist on consumer subjects, and member of the President's National Commission for Product Safety, wrote the following letter:

April 5, 1966

Mr. Paul Rand Dixon
Federal Trade Commission
Washington, D.C. 20580

Dear Mr. Dixon:

I am dismayed by the speech you gave before the Kansas City Ad Club. I am concerned about your effort to minimize high pressure selling, and to refer to people seeking legal protection against abuses in the marketplace as "zealots," and your claim that it is only a few businessmen who engage in high pressure methods.

In my experience as a reporter on consumer affairs, I don't think it is just the fringe who charge higher prices than necessary and are responsible for many of our problems. In the credit field, very often the high pressure credit sellers are financed by big respectable banks and finance companies. Nor is it the fringe sellers who are charging 18 to 22 percent for revolving credit accounts, and fighting

fiercely against the true-interest bill. It is the biggest retailers in the country.

As for deceptive and exaggerated packaging, some of it
is practiced by some of the most "reputable" big companies
in the country, whatever your word "reputable" means or
is worth.

In case you have forgotten your own experience, it is the
biggest and best known drug manufacturers who are forc-
ing the public to pay many times the manufacturing cost
for vital medicines, and still are despite the Kefauver Drug
Amendments. And it is practically all the drug manufacturers, isn't it? Not just a few? And what about the tire
jungle? Are all the exaggerated claims and deceptive
qualities, etc., just a few manufacturers, or is it practically
all the "reputable" ones?

When you speak of "zealots" seeking legislation, do you
include Senators Kefauver, Hart, Douglas, Neuberger,
Nelson and the dozens of other fine Congressmen trying
to help the consumer? Or about whom are you speaking?

I could go on, about whether it's "few" as you maintain,
or many. But it seems to me that you could have made
your points about "self restraint" without exaggerating
about "zealots for more and bigger government, trumpeting
the misdeeds of the few as an argument for more central
authority."

Sincerely,

Sidney Margolius

It is the ghetto dweller whose home has just been lost
to a fraudulent aluminum-siding swindle who knows
what real tyranny is. And it is the American housewife

exploited by games, gimmicks, and deception who is in need of protection.

The Chairman cannot honestly believe that economic forces are incapable of tyranny, and he undoubtedly realizes that government is the consumer's only viable resort for redress or for relief. Further, it is hard to believe that he is not aware, despite indications to the contrary, that the chief responsibility for these crimes must ultimately be placed on big business, not on the occasional fly-by-night operation attended to by the FTC and the Better Business Bureaus. Drugs, fake promotional games, automobiles, buses, oil depletion allowances and special tax privileges, pollution, pipelines, radiation, contaminated meat and fish, false packaging, dishonest lending practices, and many other crucial problem areas of the recent past and of the present involve big corporations primarily.

A charitable explanation of the Chairman's attitude is that it is a form of indolence. It is simply easier to ride with the tides of power and to dismiss those who question or suggest action than to take action against the economic forces so well represented in Washington. A mask is both a cover and a shield.

The act requires all affected agencies to publish in the *Federal Register* regulations implementing the new act and its policy—spelling out each agency's organizational structure and procedures, including specific procedures by which persons can gain access to information.

The Congressional analysis evaluates the implementing regulations of the various agencies required to publish them, focusing on "the degree to which they implement the law in accordance with the intent of the Congress." It concluded that

> most [agencies'] regulations . . . meet the letter and spirit of the law. A few, however, contain language showing that arrogant public-information policies still endure in agencies.

It found that the FTC's regulations are among these—and that the agency has given no indication of revising its regulations. Says the Congressional analysis:

> in a section entitled "Released Confidential Information," the FTC flouts the law by resurrecting from the prior law the phrase "for good cause shown."[1] It directs that the requester state in writing and under oath the nature of his interest and the purpose for which the information will be used if the application is granted. The section concludes: "Upon receipt of such an application the Commission will take action thereon, having due regard to statutory restrictions, its rules and the public interest." The FTC obviously fails to recognize that the [Freedom of Information] act specifically provides that persons requesting information no longer are required to state why they want it. Any information not falling under any of the law's nine categories of exemptions is deemed public information and is to be released without qualification.

This official opinion is supported by competent individuals outside the government. For example, Professor

---

[1] Technically, the Freedom of Information Act is an amendment to Section 30 of the Administrative Procedure Act, which formerly read, in pertinent part ". . . matters of official record shall . . . be made available to persons properly and directly concerned except information held confidential for good cause shown."

.m Archibald of the Missouri School of Journalism, who has done a survey of agency regulations under the Freedom of Information Act, says those of the FTC are the worst.

Secrecy

In a recent letter to Ralph Nader, dated September 27, 1968, Chairman Dixon quoted from President Johnson's statement upon signing the Freedom of Information Act on July 4, 1966:

> This legislation springs from one of our most essential principles. A democracy works best when the people have all the information that the security of the Nation permits. No one should be able to pull curtains of secrecy around decisions which can be revealed without injury to the public interest.

Our investigatory team had a three-month opportunity to observe at first hand the operation of the FTC's information policies. We were dealt with as members of the general public—not as litigants, businessmen, members of Congress, or representatives of the White House. We found that when "average citizens" seek information on consumer problems and FTC performance of regulatory duties, the agency responds with total secrecy or minimal disclosure.

To begin with, the FTC's official policy regarding what is and is not confidential, as set forth in its rules of procedure, is in blatant conflict with the Freedom of Information Act. That statute constitutes a clear Congressional command to Federal regulatory agencies to disclose to the public *all* but a limited number of kinds of information. Or, as the Congressional analysis of the act stated:

> through the act the Congress has adopted a philosophy that "any person" should have clear access to agency records without having to state a reason for wanting the information. . . . The burden of proving withholding to be necessary is placed on the Government agency.[1]

Public Documents

Sec. 4.9 of the Commission's Rules of Practice designates specific documents as "public," including the Annual Report, descriptions of FTC organization, cease and desist orders, industry guides, texts or digests of selected advisory opinions, rules, reports of FTC decisions in adjudicative proceedings, a record of votes of Commission members on every proceeding, pleadings, *published* staff and Commission reports, agreements containing consent cease and desist orders, news releases, copies of laws, *approved* compliance reports and assurances of voluntary compliance. We found that a number of these categories of documents were less public in practice than on paper. Advisory opinions are never printed in full text, for example. Only digests are made public, with no identifying details or background information. This policy precludes effective public criticism of important

---

[1] *The Freedom of Information Act, Compilation and Analysis of Departmental Regulations Implementing 5 U.S.C. 552,* 90th Congress, 2nd Session, Committee on Government Operations, 1–2 (1968).

Commission decisions, for under the agency's rules advisory opinions are binding on the Commission until revoked.

The FTC cites protection of trade secrets in refusing to divulge the identity of and information about applicants. If this were really the case then information should be withheld *only* in cases in which individual business entities seek advice, not where industry-wide trade associations apply for opinions—since presumably trade associations, generally interested in self-regulation, have little need to keep information secret. Our requests, however, for access to full texts of advisory opinions given to trade associations were consistently denied, with the exception of one opinion given to the National Association of Retail Druggists which was finally made available to us, but only, the Commission stated,

> because we have been informed that the requesting party published [the opinion] in its Journal at the time of issuance.[1]

The fate of that opinion is instructive of an additional disadvantage of advisory-opinion secrecy. Not only was it published in a trade journal, as the Commission stated, but the attorney who obtained it—former FTC Chairman Earl Kintner—shared in the publicity. This experience suggests that FTC secrecy on advisory opinions permits recipient attorneys to publicize them selectively as they choose, thus in effect marketing their dealings with government.

---

[1] Letter from Chairman Dixon to John Schulz, October 25, 1968.

Finally, if protection of trade secrets is a central concern of advisory-opinion confidentiality, there should be some sort of statute of limitations on secrecy. There is none, we learned from the Division of Advisory Opinions as well as from the Chairman himself.

Assurances of voluntary compliance and compliance reports, while generally available to the public in some sense of the word (we were assured by staff members interviewed that very few of these documents are held confidential), in fact provide minimal disclosure of information. The agency achieves this in two ways. First, the only text it permits to be made public is extremely general and conclusory—public assurances of voluntary compliance and compliance reports both contain only language like "X.Y.Z. has ceased to carry on its business in the manner disapproved of and will not do so again." All *detailed* communications from challenged businessmen, the real meat of such cases, are held absolutely confidential. Second, to say that these texts are made "public" is to stretch the meaning of the word: a single copy of each is placed in ring-binders in the docket room of the agency's central office building in Washington. But no copies are made or distributed to anyone and no news releases on them are issued.[1] In other words, there is little likelihood that the public will ever learn of a businessman's transgression. The handling of these rec-

---

[1] Except that, in the case of assurances, a release appears every few months which summarizes *very* briefly all assurances accepted in the previous few months. These summaries typically tell only how many assurances have been received—usually 80 to 90—then give about three very brief examples of problems involved without identifying any respondent.

ords provides an example of partial secrecy at the FTC. As such, it permits the agency to proclaim (when challenged) that such information is public while effectively keeping it from the general public.

Other examples of partial secrecy at the FTC involve consent orders and news releases. Proposed consent orders are made "public" without publicity—a single copy is placed at the central office; they remain public for thirty days. As for news releases, even when they are issued about deceptive-practice cases, for example, they are typically so laced with opaque legalisms that, even in the opinion of members of the trade press, it is difficult to extract any usable information from them. If reporters trained in the field can't get the message, how can consumers?

A final example of limited publicity is the Commission's handling of the transcripts of such important "public hearings" as those held in 1968 on consumer protection. The normal practice is for the Commission to purchase *one* copy of a hearing transcript and place it in the docket room of its central office in Washington. In one earlier case, the tire hearings of January, 1965, the agency made a single additional copy available at its Chicago field office because of extreme public pressure. Chairman Dixon refused to print the hearing record, saying that the FTC's contract with Ward & Paul, stenographers, precluded it. Of course, any interested, affluent citizen can purchase his own copy of any hearing transcript from Ward & Paul at only 50 cents a page.

Confidential Information

The Commission's rules specify certain rather broad categories of matters that it deems specifically confidential. These categories are roughly those defined as exemptions in the Freedom of Information Act. The three categories used by the FTC are trade secrets, "internal communications," and matters under "investigation."

We found that in practice the Commission appeals broadly and woodenly to these categories to support nondisclosure of various kinds of documentary information, and that it uses other tactics to avoid disclosure of agency records.

Trade Secrets

FTC policy here is illustrated by attempts made over the last few years by Professor Kenneth Culp Davis of the University of Chicago, author of a four-volume treatise on administrative law, to secure Commission disclosure of samples of pre-merger clearances issued by the FTC.

Professor Davis's ordeal began in August, 1966, when he visited Chairman Dixon and requested to examine Commission files showing clearances for mergers. Mr. Dixon refused, suggesting a request by letter, which Professor Davis obligingly made in November. In December, he made a revised request, limited to the files of *"the three latest cases* in which the Commission has granted clearance for merger." On January 13, 1967, Chairman Dixon responded, agreeing to make public only *digests* of pre-merger matters, on the specific analogy of advisory opinions. Professor Davis wrote back immediately expressing his dissatisfaction as a scholar:

> . . . [publication of digests] does not meet my need to examine the files. You are quite right in saying that I want to know the law and policy of the Commission with respect to such clearances, but such digests clearly will not suffice.

He then repeated his request, stressing the nature of his interest:

> My purpose is wholly scholarly. I have absolutely no interest in the kind of business facts a corporation wants kept confidential . . . ; such facts can be taken out of the files I examine. My lifetime project is to try to understand the administrative process . . .

This letter was apparently ignored, and Professor Davis sent two follow-up letters in October and one in November, 1967, requesting "permission to examine Commission files showing interpretations made in pre-merger clearances during 1966 and 1967." Finally, on November 27, 1967, came the Commission's single-spaced three-page response—denying Professor Davis's request. In this letter, pre-merger clearances have been fully conceptualized as advisory opinions, and the agency goes on record as exceptionally protective of information handed over to it by parties who approach it voluntarily, thus:

. . . parties who approach the agency in this posture [voluntarily] are entitled to an even greater degree of protection than those against whom it has been necessary to invoke mandatory procedures for no law compels them to come in and make the disclosures they make. Instead they do so of their own free will in order to avail themselves of the services which the agency affords, secure in the knowledge that the secrets which they voluntarily unfold will be held in strictest confidence by the public agency. . . .

But Commissioner Elman disagreed, convincingly, in a separate statement:

In my view, there is no substantial interest which would be harmed by letting Professor Davis examine these materials. Professor Davis is not asking to see any correspondence or records which the Commission secured under a pledge they would be kept secret.

Professor Davis answered on November 29, 1967, citing relevant provisions of the Freedom of Information Act and commenting that he intended to bring the matter to the attention of various other governmental agencies if not satisfied with the Commission's handling of the matter. This produced a bristling Commission response dated December 15, 1967, in which Professor Davis's view of the Freedom of Information Act was hotly rejected and the following statement appeared:

In closing, the Commission wishes to add one or two other observations. While it feels that there must somewhere be an end to this dialogue, you may be assured that it is also our desire to have you work with us rather than against us and that the Commission has here evidenced a wish to cooperate with you in every way it properly can. A great number of our top level personnel has spent a great deal of time in making available to you all the information which could be released and the Commission itself has spent an unusual amount of time in considering this individual request because it considered the matter to be important and because it wished to cooperate with you in the work you are doing. But it is evident that cooperation involves considerable give and take on both sides and not the complete capitulation of one side to the other. Certainly, this Commission will not be forced into that sort of cooperation by undisguised threats that request will be made for Congressional action, which are not to be expected from one of your outstanding reputation and which the Commission cannot believe were intended in the manner stated.

Once again, Commissioner Elman disagreed, stating that he

does not regard Professor Davis's letter . . . as carrying any "threats." A citizen has the right to bring matters of public concern to the attention of interested committees of Congress. No government agency should feel threatened by such a proposed course of action.

Not yet discouraged, Professor Davis sent another letter on January 2, 1968, focusing on merger files containing no confidential information, and making a new, more limited request:

I request access to the Commission's pre-merger files to the extent of examining the names of corporations involved in applications for pre-merger clearances, and only to that extent.

The Chairman's response, January 18, 1968, was another denial, stating, among other things:

Certainly, the question of disclosure of the names of corporations involved . . . is undoubtedly the most confidential information of all and would be the very last thing the Commission would make public.

On February 20, 1968, Professor Davis wrote again, this time appealing to the whole Commission with regard to the Chairman's letter of January 18, 1968, arguing his case on the basis of the Freedom of Information Act, and requesting only "those papers in the clearance files that are not within one of the nine exemptions to the Information Act."

This approach was equally unsuccessful—on April 30, 1968, the Commission informed the professor that it had once more denied his request (Commissioner Elman dissenting), emphasizing once again the need to extend confidential treatment of voluntary submissions by businessmen.

At this point, Professor Davis gave up, at least for now, sadder but wiser about the realities of the administrative process.

Internal Communications

During the course of our study we learned that a series of staff memoranda existed providing a rather complete breakdown of applications for complaint received by the FTC (containing such figures as total numbers of complaints received, numbers from various sources, numbers from various categories of applicants, numbers by state, and so on).

Copies of these memos were requested from Monroe Day, the administrative officer, who prepares them. He stated that he had been told not to give us any information. We then approached the Chairman, who denied our request, reciting the "inter-agency memorandum" exemption to the Freedom of Information Act. We responded that these particular memoranda did not seem to contain the sort of information which justifies that exemption (e.g., critical, evaluative comments; notes of plans, tactics, etc.—information which agency personnel would be loathe to include in memos if they were public); these memos, in contrast, contain only objective factual data. The Chairman was unimpressed; repeating the phrase "inter-agency memoranda," he refused again.

Copies of these memoranda were eventually made available by Commission action after we had filed formal request.

We encountered two other information problems which involve agency memoranda. One was a single case of refusal by FTC staff and the Chairman to *identify* certain specific documents in the Commission's possession sufficiently to permit a subsequent request for access to them. This sort of ploy is a problem since the Freedom of Information Act and FTC rules require disclosure only of "identifiable records." The Attorney General's Memorandum analyzing the act, however, makes it clear that

agencies should not try to avoid disclosing documents by
refusing to identify them where the requesting party
gives a reasonably specific description of what he wants.
Says the Memorandum: "This requirement of identification is not to be used as a method of withholding records." [1]

The requirement was so used in this case. Because we
could not identify the records in question (certain compliance files whose exact form we did not know), we
could not include them in our formal request to the
Commission for data, and they have never been disclosed.

The other problem, somewhat related, is really as
much a matter of information policy. Briefly, the FTC
fails to keep accurate records of its performance. It is
thus able to turn down requests for relevant information
for the extraordinary reason that it has no information on
the topics of interest and that to process basic data in
order to produce such information would be either impossible or prohibitively expensive. We encountered this
phenomenon several times, but the clearest example was
the Commission's response to certain demands for information made in a formal request submitted to the agency
under Section 4.11 of its rules. This request, made September 30, 1968, by letter under oath from John Schulz
to Chairman Dixon included the following questions [2]

---

[1] *Attorney General's Memorandum,* p. 23. (Quoting Senate Report
on the Act, p. 8.)

[2] Modeled on identical questions asked in 1964 of the Commission
by Senator Gordon Allott of Colorado about the Bureau of Restraint
of Trade. Senator Allott's questions were answered, suggesting that the

about enforcement costs in the Bureau of Deceptive Practices:

Question 6.

What are the total expenditures which have been allocated to the prosecution (and/or handling) of these matters [deceptive-practice matters in litigation, consent settlement, informal disposition, under investigation for guides, etc.] up to the present time?

Question 7.

What is the present status of each of these matters and what additional funds does the Commission anticipate will be required to resolve each of these cases, assuming respondents (participants) exhaust all administrative and judicial remedies?

Previous answers indicate that the total number of matters in each category is very small; for example, 24 cases in litigation, 23 pending consent settlement, 29 pending informal settlement, etc. Yet the Commission's response of October 25 to questions 6 and 7 was:

Question 6.

The basic information is available from the Commission's Time and Action data. . . . However, in order to compile the information requested, the Commission staff would be required to write at least four computer programs. Several days of machine time would also be

Commission's response to our request overstates things a bit and that the FTC does not treat citizens the same way it treats members of the Senate Committee on Commerce.

required. This would require at least ten man days of work.

Question 7.

The basic information is *not presently available*. Because of the many variables involved, the Commission has not been successful in the past in accurately anticipating total costs.

It seems that this sort of information should have a high priority because of its usefulness for cost-benefit analysis.

Needless to say, failure to keep adequate files and records is more the responsibility of the staff heads than the Commissioners. In fact, even the Commissioners occasionally discover that information in which they are interested does not exist or cannot be retrieved because of inadequate record-keeping. For example, in April, 1967, the Commission directed its staff to submit a report on the agency's experience with insurance cases over the last five years, including among other things, "the number of complaints received." Responded the staff:

Number of Complaints Received

The basic information for this item is contained primarily in the closed preliminary correspondence files in the Division of Legal Records. These files are not indexed as to subject matter and include anti-trust as well as deceptive practice matters, general inquiries and other types of letters as well as complaints. Thus, to extract the letters containing complaints regarding insurance would require an individual examination of the entire number filed over the last five years. Figures from the Records Division show that the total number of all closed preliminary files have averaged about 5,000 per year, which amounts to a total of some 25,000 files since January 1, 1962. In addition there are complaints on insurance, much fewer in number which are contained in the closed files of the Bureau of Industry Guidance.[1]

Investigatory Files

The exemption regarding investigatory files included in the Freedom of Information Act is used most by the FTC to cloak its activities in secrecy, for the agency treats *every* kind of investigation as being within the exemption. Thus, for example, whether we requested information concerning matters under preliminary investigation (which are carried on from the time an application for complaint is received from a member of the public to the time the Commission issues a complaint), matters under investigation for compliance with outstanding orders, or matters under investigation leading to issuance of industry guides, etc., the constant response of the staff and Chairman was, "no disclosure—investigatory files." This interpretation of the Freedom of Information Act is so broad as to permit the agency nearly to evade that Act entirely. In addition, since the Commission is free to disclose *even* information exempted from mandatory disclosure, its policy with respect to investigatory files represents a consistent slighting of consumer interests in favor of business

[1] Memorandum to Commission from William S. Hill, Att'y, Bureau of Deceptive Practices, June 21, 1967, p. 1.

interests. When coupled with the fact that some of the longest delays in FTC administrative action occur at the "investigation" stage, the agency's confidential handling of all investigations is highly damaging to thousands of unknowing persons.

Collusion

> Collusion: . . . A secret arrangement between two or more persons, whose interests are apparently conflicting, to make use of the forms and proceedings of law in order to defraud a third person, or to obtain that which justice would not give them . . . (*Black's Law Dictionary*, p. 371.)

The FTC in this sense is engaged in active and continuing collusion with business interests—particularly big-business interests. The collusion is not the conspiratorial brand that the word often connotes. There are probably not an inordinate number of secret "deals" with kickbacks. But this is almost unfortunate, because the kind of collusion that has evolved is far more dangerous —and far more absolute. It is a collusion that can be inferred from the sociological facts of Commission and staff life. Commissioners and staff members do not live, generally, in university or ghetto environments, but in middle-class suburban areas. They associate with other government officials and come into contact most and are most interested in people who have common concerns and related occupations. This almost necessarily means a great deal of contact with and a great number of friendships with businessmen, other government workers, attorneys, and Congressmen. The Commissioners have very little personal contact with the aggrieved consumer. His complaint, if it is expressed at all, takes the form of an impersonal letter.

To some extent their acquaintances among businessmen are responsible for the reliance of FTC members on the businessman's presumptive honesty, even in situations where an honest man might falter.

Not only is there close communication and contact among these groups, but there is actual interchange of jobs. Indeed, many of the young attorneys in the Commission staff view their experience as training for later corporate work. Their acquaintances among the staff and Commission serve them well in this capacity and multiply their contacts and communications with business interests.

Recently two other agencies saw their top political officials leave to take high positions in the industries they previously regulated. This is a common phenomenon in Washington and is especially prevalent in the case of the FTC because of the potential power of the Commission in the regulation of business generally.

The attorney plays a crucial role in the acculturation process in Washington. He is the middleman, the cover. Washington law firms specialize in regulatory work and carefully nurture friendships with Commission and staff personnel. Their advantages in accomplishing their mission are immense. They are highly paid and better trained than the FTC attorneys with whom they will deal. They have the attorney-client privilege to justify a tradition of secrecy. They have the advantage of numerous Congressional and White House contacts, which they can use by implication to deter or intimidate staff members. They have the advantage, finally, of holding a covey of IOU's which they can call in as the interests of their clients require.

The acculturation process as applied to the FTC is particularly intense. It is common procedure for trade associations to wine and dine influential staff personnel. To understand the result, consider the work of Duke Wilson, chief of the Division of General Trade Restraints. He is known around the Commission as the darling of the retail gas dealers' trade association and has awards from the association to prove it. He has earned his reputation by immediately investigating independent dealers for "price discrimination" when they lower prices below the established level for their market.

The Commissioners themselves and particularly the Chairman are not free from the process. The most frightening thing about this situation is the fact that the people involved do not seem to know what is happening, that they do not even know they are out of touch and even blind to certain elements of society. Chairman Dixon, for example, gives many speeches and is invited to numerous banquets. At one of them recently he opened his speech by saying:

> Sometimes I think that Washington is too far from any-place. That's why I think it's a good idea to get out into the rest of the country to find out first hand what is worrying people, or what they are shrugging off as unimportant.

These remarks were contained in a speech to the Advertising Club of New Orleans on May 16, 1967. Mr. Dixon has traveled outside Washington a great deal, delivering some 109 formal speeches, the great majority of them to trade associations.[1] Mr. Dixon has carried his culture with him. He has spoken almost exclusively to those he associates with generally, businessmen and related legal interests. It would be from their point of view that Chairman Dixon judges the "unimportant" matters he is "shrugging off."

In a sense what happens to the Commissioners and staff members is not active collusion. Long, amicable exposure to those they are supposed to regulate has given them a perspective more sympathetic to business interests than to consumers. The FTC, in effect, becomes the very thing it is designed to regulate. The evolution of Commission personality is particularly marked in an agency whose Chairman and core staff have been under the constant influence of their subculture for a number of years. Chairman Dixon has served longer than any other chairman, and his appointment does not expire until 1974.

Given this state of affairs, it is not surprising that business interests do not show much respect for the threat of FTC enforcement. Edward Wimmer, Vice President of the National Federation of Independent Business, submitted an affidavit to the Federal Trade Commission on behalf of a gas-station owner who had been threatened

---

[1] Of 109 speeches, trade associations or advertisers totaled 62; antitrust sections of bar associations (pro-business), 21; universities, 8; consumer groups, 2; miscellaneous (Better Business Bureaus, etc.), 16.

and heavily pressured by S&H Trading Stamp representatives. Mr. Wimmer wrote:

> I know your files are packed with affidavits and other findings similar to this testimony, but it keeps going on and on. Every time I run into a stamp man, he gives us the laugh when we mention that the Federal Trade Commission is going to do something about this "business."

The FTC favors business also with its so-called industry-wide enforcement tools—industry guides and trade-regulation rules. The argument for these "voluntary" enforcement tools was presented to us by William B. Snow, Jr., assistant chief for the Commission's Bureau of Industry Guidance, which administers them. Because it would not be fair, he explained, to challenge only one of many businessmen engaging in a particular widespread deception, an industry-wide approach should be used to stop all violators at the same time. This view is not without plausibility. But it neglects fairness to consumers. As we have seen in the tire-advertising guides, actual FTC handling of industry-wide tools produces poor results—poorer even than the agency's use of "individual" tools. In its solicitousness for the welfare of a law-breaking businessman, the FTC permits him and others to continue to cause damage to thousands of innocent consumers.

There is a final example of the FTC's unhealthy friendliness to business interests in those cases where the Commission is more lenient than industry self-regulatory groups.

One such involves the broadcast industry, whose advertising practices are simultaneously under the jurisdiction of the FTC Act and the Codes of the National Association of Broadcasters. An official of the association interviewed on August 21, 1968, told us that media advertisers frequently seek advisory opinions from the Commission to avoid the more stringent provisions of the broadcasters' code. They reason, he said, that "if the FTC says we can do it, the NAB can't stop us." Other advertisers apply to the FTC for industry guides or trade-regulation rules, knowing that the case will bog down in a typical FTC swamp of delay, during which they can defy the broadcasters' codes with the excuse that the FTC has "taken jurisdiction." The ultimate rule or guide will, of course, be easier to live with than the industry code.

Apparently, the mask "works," but there is no respect for the agency behind it. One soon learns that there is little substance to the unhealthy exterior.

V

THE CANCER

IT IS UNWRITTEN gospel in Washington, in academia, and in business that personalities or even individuals should not be discussed publicly. To name names is somehow to "cheapen" criticism. To talk about the individuals who take action or who fail to act is considered bad taste, distracting, and irrelevant. This is why it is safe to predict that many will criticize the "style" of our evaluation—though the same persons will probably say that our thesis and documentation are convincing. But the evaluation would bring very little response at all if it did not discuss the people involved— not their private lives—but the impact of their personalities and values on their public responsibilities. There is a certain amount of hypocrisy in the criticism of this approach because *everyone* who deals with the Federal Trade Commission discusses these factors privately. Law firms even keep files on the predilections and personal prejudices of FTC personnel.

We propose to analyze the real problem of this Federal agency—not through the cloak of abstraction—but openly, frankly, and systematically. The real problem of the FTC —and indeed of any faltering agency—can usually be traced to *people*. Misguided leadership is the malignant cancer that has already assumed control of the Commission, that has been silently destroying it, and that has spread its contagion on the growing crisis of the American consumer.

We propose to consider the nature and makeup of the FTC, who controls it, how and why, and for what purposes. We shall review partisan political activity and relations—or arrangements—with Congress. Then we shall take a look at the Commission's collective background, its treatment of minorities, its hiring practices, and occupational biases.

Partisan Politics

The official image of the Federal Trade Commission is, as it should be, a nonpolitical agency that regulates interstate commerce against anticompetitive and unfair practices in the public interest. To insulate the agency from party politics, the original FTC law stipulated that no more than three Commissioners could be from the same political party. And the Commissioners' tenures were limited to seven years, with their appointment staggered. Beyond this the Hatch Act of 1964 prohibits the soliciting of political funds by government employees. In a further safeguard, the Civil Service Commission forbids party discrimination in hiring.

Yet in the case of the present regime at the FTC, the Hatch Act and the Civil Service Law are treated as mere rhetoric. Most attorneys at the FTC are labeled as either Democrat or Republican, and their party affiliation has a definite bearing on the positions they are offered. All staff attorneys at the FTC from bureau chief to executive director hold their positions on appointment from Chairman Dixon who, in effect, may replace them whenever he desires and reduce them from a supergrade to a GS-15.[1] Ideally, the Chairman rotates the FTC staff to place the best men at the top of each operating bureau. When Mr. Dixon became Chairman in 1960, it seems that the "best men" were all Democrats. Any Republican in a high position was offered the choice of becoming a trial lawyer at the bottom of the organization chart or resigning.

As a result, fourteen highly experienced career men left the Commission almost immediately. In its November 20, 1961, issue, *Advertising Age* called partisan politics the major reason for a shake-up at the FTC. As a result, the magazine said, the quality of key personnel had deteriorated. In time most of the Republicans found it hard to swallow their pride and left. A few able ones, such as the former Assistant Executive Director, Basil

---

[1] The GS ratings are the official grade scale ranks for civil-service employees. They determine pay and often power within Federal agencies. The professional scale extends from GS-9 to GS-18. GS-16, 17, and 18 are referred to as "supergrade" appointments, that is, they are not permanent but political positions. The holder of a supergrade can be reduced to a GS-15 at the will of the chairman.

Mezines, and John Walker, an attorney, have stuck it out. Throughout this time, however, being "out" men has grown increasingly uncomfortable.

Of the nearly 500 lawyers working for the Commission only some forty are now Republicans, about twenty of them in the central office. Only one Republican holds a position of any prominence in the operating bureaus of the FTC: Charles Moore, who recently succeeded Sam Williams as chief of the Bureau of Field Operations. Mr. Moore is a Republican, but in his case there is an extenuating factor—he comes from Johnson City, Tennessee. There are advantages for the ambitious at the FTC in being born in Tennessee or, for that matter, in any small town in the South. There is a popular story around the Commission, which, if not true in fact is certainly true to the spirit of the FTC, going back to the late Depression years in which the story is set. At that time, Boss Crump's Memphis machine had control of FTC patronage through the services of Commissioner Edwin C. Davis, a protege of Crump's. The Memphis boss sent the Commission a state legislator who had just failed to be re-elected. His name was Fletcher Cohn. While Commissioner Davis was considering where to place Mr. Cohn, a staff delegation came to see him. "But Judge," said their spokesman, "don't you know that . . . why, er, Fletcher Cohn, he's Jewish." The Commission had never had a Jewish attorney on its staff before. Nonetheless, Commissioner Davis took the news calmly, withering the delegation with his reply: "But he come from Tennessee, don' he?"

Besides permitting his staff to violate the spirit and the

letter of the Civil Service Law in promotion and hiring, Chairman Dixon himself has violated the Hatch Act. Highly reliable sources at the FTC revealed that until recently Mr. Dixon was notorious for dunning the agency's personnel as far down as the GS-14 level for political contributions. This group includes approximately one-quarter of the more than 300 lawyers working in the central office in Washington. The chief collector of dues used to be that same Mr. Cohn, who now holds the title of Assistant General Counsel for Legislation. Mr. Dixon's reputation with Democratic party fund raisers is reported to be excellent. It is also known in the high echelons of the Commission that Chairman Dixon is openly proud of his fund raising. His methods would make any chairman of an alumni fund-raising committee jealous. Members of the staff have testified to receiving solicitation cards from the Democratic National Committee with a code number in the corner which everyone involved knew would indicate to Chairman Dixon who gave and who did not. This method was not well received by those who were being coerced into giving against their will. Eventually, the threat of action by the Justice Department under the Hatch Act forced Chairman Dixon to give up open political exploitation of his employees. He now uses more discreet methods. For example, he personally asks his subordinates to buy $100-a-plate tickets to Democratic fund-raising dinners. Thus Chairman Dixon persists in playing partisan politics, while neglecting his responsibilities as a public servant.[1]

---

[1] After we released our original report, a Washington correspondent for *The St. Louis Post-Dispatch* made an independent investigation of

Friends on Capitol Hill

Even more destructive to the sense of purpose and nonpolitical ideal of the Commission are the Congressional politics that permeate it. Congressional pressures have made nonsense of priorities for action which relate only in theory to the importance of the social issue involved.

According to Joseph W. Shea, Secretary of the FTC, any letter the Commission gets from a Congressman's office is specially marked with an "expedite" sticker. The sticker gives the letter high priority, assuring the Congressman of an answer within five days. No distinction is made between letters—whether from complaining constituents, which Congressmen routinely "buck" over to the FTC, or those from the Congressmen themselves. The FTC receives approximately 110 letters a month from Congressmen, only a few of them originating in the Congressman's office. Yet all these letters are answered in detail by younger members of the staff for whom this is a type of busywork. As one attorney remarked, "A letter comes in from a Congressman, and everyone drops whatever they are doing and takes care of it. . . . Great importance is attached by the higher staff to answering

---

his own and wrote an article headlined, "Solicitation of Staff Admitted by Dixon." According to the article, Chairman Dixon "defended the practice, saying that it was legal as long as the solicitation came from outside the agency and as long as there was no coercion. . . ." Other informed sources told *The Post-Dispatch*, however, that Dixon's lieutenants actively solicited the political payments by visiting employees in their offices and calling meetings in the agency to inquire whether they had made their contributions.

these letters fully and properly. . . . How can you do a job with that kind of continual interruption?"

All matters that Congressmen deem important are handled by telephone or in person. These cordial personal contacts are constant. They are also more than casual. One lawyer in the Bureau of Deceptive Practices commented candidly, "Everyone who wants to go anywhere at the FTC has a political connection." He then unblushingly named a Congressman who was his own sponsor.

The personal influence of Congressmen begins at the top. Chairman Dixon was appointed by President Kennedy under heavy pressure from the late Senator Estes Kefauver—of Tennessee. The runner-up for the chairmanship, A. Everette MacIntyre, was sponsored by Representative Wright Patman of Texas. He was given the next available Commissioner's post as a consolation prize. Casual scrutiny of the FTC reveals a number of other political sponsors. One day we were fortunate enough to find William Jibb, director of the FTC's Office of Information, at his desk. (According to reporters who deal with the Office of Information regularly, Mr. Jibb is rarely there. We also found this to be true. Wilbur Weaver, Mr. Jibb's assistant, seems to be able to run the office quite well apparently without aid from Mr. Jibb.) Mr. Jibb insisted on telling us that he had been an old college friend and political aide of Senator G. Smathers of Florida.

Other members of the Commission's staff are less talkative about their political connections, which are nonetheless well known—Joseph W. Shea's for example. Mr.

Shea comes from Boston, and his official title, stated in his biography, is "Secretary and Congressional Liaison Officer." The Commission telephone book and budget-control reports list him simply as "Secretary." His biography also notes "came to Washington, D.C., April 19, 1934, under sponsorship of Speaker John W. McCormack as a clerk at $1,000 per annum and attended evening law school." Around the Federal Trade Commission he is known "to be like a son" to the Speaker of the House. His biography notes mysteriously that he "has accrued sick leave of 2,211 hours and maximum annual leave," a piece of information not usually placed in FTC biographies. The 1965 Civil Service Commission study of FTC management practices seemed disturbed by this fact and the very high supergrade of GS-16 with a salary of $25,875 that Mr. Shea held. Their report stated:

> The Secretary's position was placed in grade GS-16 upon the statements of the Chairman regarding the personal contributions the Secretary has made to the Commission through his highly successful personal contacts outside the Commission. Personal contributions of this nature do not permit their delegation to subordinates in the principal's absence. The other responsibilities of the Secretary—i.e., the preparation of the Minutes and maintaining the official records of the Commission—were not factors influencing the classification of this position.[1] (p. 48)

Other officers in high positions at the FTC have political contacts or relations similar to Mr. Shea's. John W.

---

[1] Civil Service Commission.

Brookfield (GS-15, $22,695), the chief of the Division of Food and Drug Advertising in the Bureau of Deceptive Practices, is the nephew of the former Chairman of the House Rules Committee, Representative Howard W. Smith. Fletcher Cohn is now a GS-16 earning $24,477. According to Richard Harrington of *The Washington Post*, March 27, 1966, Mr. Cohn is "the FTC's lobbyist and Ambassador to Capitol Hill." Cecil G. Miles (GS-17, $26,960) is a close acquaintance of a fellow Arkansan, Representative Wilbur D. Mills. He is also bureau chief in the Bureau of Restraint of Trade. The list goes on, but the conclusion is obvious—if you want to float to the top of the FTC, a political friend is the most beautiful buoy in the world.

Perhaps the Congressman with the most influence in the decisions of the FTC is Representative Joe Evins—of Tennessee—who is also Chairman of the House Appropriations Subcommittee, which approves the FTC's budget. One staff member of the FTC stated the rule: "Ambitious staff attorneys at the FTC who are from Tennessee have to know Joe Evins." For example, when a political friend, Judge Casto C. Geer, wanted to work near his home town in Tennessee, the FTC obligingly set up an office in Oak Ridge, although it does not have any offices in, for instance, Detroit or Philadelphia. Although the FTC never announced the opening of its new office, Representative Evins did make an announcement which, together with a picture of Judge Geer, appeared on the front page of *The Chattanooga Times*.

Bill Weaver of the FTC Office of Information discovered the new branch of the FTC only from casual conversation with people in the supply room who were shipping office equipment to Oak Ridge. Even two of the Commissioners were unaware of the Oak Ridge branch until informed by sources outside the Commission. In addition, Judge Geer is the only FTC field operative anywhere in the country not listed under the Bureau of Field Operations, but directly responsible to the Bureau of Deceptive Practices, which is directed by Chairman Dixon's close friend, Frank Hale. In a telephone interview Mr. Hale could not say precisely what kind of work occupied Judge Geer, adding parenthetically "but I understand there's a good deal of work down there." A telephone interview with the Judge himself proceeded as follows:

Interviewer: What date was the Oak Ridge Office opened?

Judge Geer: You will have to get that information from the central office.

Interviewer: What type of work primarily occupies you?

Judge Geer: You will have to get that information from the central office.

Interviewer: You mean to say that they know more about your work in Washington than you do in Oak Ridge?

Judge Geer: Well, they have the first hand information there.

(pause)

Interviewer: Is it an FTC policy to release all information only through the central office?

Judge Geer: (pause) I don't know if it is or not.

Interviewer: On what grounds, then, do you refuse to give even the most innocuous information?

Judge Geer: You will have to get that information from the central office.

Since the Office of Information did not know about the Oak Ridge office, we talked directly to the Executive Director, John Wheelock. He went into a long explanation of why the Oak Ridge office was attached to the Atlanta field office instead of the Cleveland office ("Very few attorneys like to serve in Cleveland because of the weather"). Even this explanation, as subsequent investigation showed, was false. Judge Geer continuous to collect his salary of $17,500.

When the FTC wanted an economist for its Division of Economic Evidence, it selected Harrison F. Houghton, the chief economist from Joe Evins's Select Committee on Small Business. Mr. Houghton has subsequently been made Acting Director of the Bureau of Economics.

Not that all Congressional pressure is bad. The FTC has reacted to the demands of such men from the Hill as Senator Warren Magnuson and Representative Benjamin Rosenthal of New York. The results were investigations into important issues—insurance frauds, home-improvement frauds, deceptive auto warranties, and deleterious frozen foods. In all these cases the FTC should have known enough to act earlier on its own.

Unseen influences from other Congressmen, however, have had other effects. Sometimes they amount simply to the misallocation of scarce resources for a small investigation in a Congressman's home district. In other cases, such as the opening of the Oak Ridge office, there are gross misallocations of public funds. Most horrifying, however, are those cases where the influence of a Congressman can actually present a danger to human life.

Such was the case of the flammable baby blankets. In the 1950's Representative Albert Thomas of Texas was Chairman of the House Subcommittee on Appropriations for Independent Agencies, the post now held by Joe Evins. Representative Thomas, on behalf of Texas cotton interests, influenced the Commission to rule that baby blankets were not covered by the Flammable Fabrics Law. Baby blankets, the Commission said, do not qualify as "clothing."

"Like a Southern County Courthouse"

Party politics and Congressional ties, which have effectively vitiated the work the FTC should be doing, are symptoms of the Commission hierarchy's collective personality.

During the pro-business days of the Republican administrations of the 1920's, the FTC, for lack of any other use, became a dumping ground for political patronage. President Roosevelt, recognizing the FTC's potential, tried to reform its personnel and use it to spearhead his New Deal program. However, his attempts to remove the worst of the Commissioners was rebuffed in 1935 by the Supreme Court in the case of *U.S. v. Humphrey's Executor*, on the grounds that a Commissioner's position was quasi-judicial. Roosevelt gave up on the FTC and used it to his political advantage by granting it as a political dukedom to Senator Kenneth McKellar of Tennessee. The dukedom was managed for McKellar and "Boss" Crump's Memphis political machine by another Tennessean, Commissioner Edwin C. Davis, from 1933 to 1949.[1] Throughout this period, positions were openly given because of personal connections and political patronage, with southern Democrats receiving the lion's share.

The Republican years from 1952 to 1960, were lean years for Tennesseans at the FTC, but they managed to survive, and, with a Democratic administration and Mr. Dixon's appointment, things were back to normal. Most of the top staff now at the Commission either came during the period of the "Tennessee gang" or are clubhouse friends. As one disgruntled observer stated to a *Wall Street Journal* reporter in 1963, "The atmosphere of the agency was like a southern county courthouse, and it is again." From what we saw, nothing has changed since.

As a result the men who control the FTC are simply incapable of understanding the complex problems and processes of our urban society. A symptomatic problem indicative of this point was revealed by a singularly capable GS-15 at the Commission. He was amazed that his colleagues had no knowledge of record-keeping procedures in large corporations. Our interviews with the personnel in the Records Division revealed that none of the staff has yet recognized the worth of the computer. The 1965 Civil Service Report on the FTC recognized this as a problem. The report suggested that Chairman Dixon's administration

---

[1] Commissioner Davis distinguished himself by making an annual gift to Congress of appropriated funds that had not been utilized. In a dubious tradition, this parsimonious spirit and desire to please by economy continues under Chairman Dixon and is particularly apparent in his annual testimony to Congress at appropriations time.

provide for a comprehensive study of the use of the computer in order that it may be brought into full productive use in providing:

1. Management data essential to manpower control, utilization, and planning.
2. Program resource data which will result in either increased productivity or reduced manpower requirements.

Chairman Dixon has still not instituted a comprehensive study of the sort called for by the Civil Service Commission Report.

It is the hierarchy essentially that decides priorities, selects cases to investigate, moves to issue complaints, and weighs the tactics and legal weaponry for each case. By law, Chairman Dixon (who comes from Nashville, Tennessee; population: 170,874) has general responsibility for overseeing and planning the work of the staff. His chief-of-staff is the Executive Director, John Wheelock (Spring City, Tennessee; population: under 2,500), but the assistant to the Chairman, John Buffington (Castleberry, Alabama; population: under 2, 500) acts as Chairman Dixon's liaison man and watchdog for the work of the Executive Director. Beneath Wheelock are the six bureau chiefs. The Bureau of Economics, headed by Joe Evins's ex-economist, Harrison F. Houghton (Des Moines, Iowa; population: 282,902), is the only operating bureau that does not hire lawyers for substantially all its staff. The five attorney bureau chiefs are:

Cecil G. Miles (Prairie County, Arkansas; population: 10,515) Bureau of Restraint of Trade

Frank Hale (Madisonville, Texas; population: under 2,500) Bureau of Deceptive Practices

Chalmers B. Yarley (Waterboro, South Carolina; population: 5,417) Bureau of Industry Guidance

Charles R. Moore (Johnson City, Tennessee; population: under 2,500) Bureau of Field Offices

Henry D. Stringer (Winfield, Texas; population: under 2,500) Bureau of Textiles and Furs

There are two offices made up entirely of lawyers that are also influential in making Commission policy. The Office of the General Counsel is headed by James McI. Henderson (Daingerfield, Texas; population: 3,133). The Director of the Office of Hearing Examiners is Luther Edward Creel (Alberville, Alabama; population: 8,251). Although there are thirty-five assistant bureau chiefs and division chiefs, only fifteen biographies were available from the Commission's Office of Information. Of those fifteen, nine have a small-town southern background. In the field offices there is a reverse carpetbagger effect. The attorney in charge of the Kansas City office comes from Bowdon, Georgia (population: under 2,500). The attorney in charge of the Los Angeles office transferred from Atlanta, and the attorney in charge of the San Francisco office comes from Virginia.

This common background among FTC policy makers perhaps explains why the Commission did not start to police the exploitation of the ghetto poor in the District of Columbia until late 1965, and then only because of constant prodding by Senator Warren Magnuson (Seattle, Washington) and Commissioner Mary Gardiner Jones (New York City).

If the FTC had started a vigorous consumer-protection program for the District area in 1960 instead of the weak program of 1965, perhaps a major cause of the Washington riots would have been removed. Such action, however, would have required social concern, imagination, and foresight—the very qualities inhibited in a group of people lacking diversity. A small clique of lawyers with an identical background far removed from many of the most important issues of the day should not have control over an institution with the responsibilities of the Federal Trade Commission.

The clubhouse ambience in the hierarchy interacts with political connections to produce an aversion for upsetting friends on Capitol Hill by any radical moves. For this reason Commissioner Dixon and Commissioner MacIntyre objected to a proposal that the Commission publicize housing discrimination by investigating newspaper advertising that discriminates by deception.

Chairman Dixon's attitude has been similar in the hiring of persons from minority groups. The figures in the Appendix, Section 11, are from the *Study of Minority Group Employment in the Federal Government*, prepared annually by the Civil Service Commission. The figures show that the FTC has not been averse to hiring Negroes, but only "in their place," i.e. the lowest GS 1–4 positions. The absence of changes since mid-1965 in the proportion of Negroes in the GS 5–8 levels indicates that Chairman Dixon has not encouraged the promotion of

Negroes to supervisory positions. The GS 5–8 grades comprise trained clerical help, and it would be reasonable to expect equal-opportunity hiring to produce a proportion of Negroes somewhat higher than one-sixth the proportion of Negroes in the Washington population. The 1965 Civil Service Report on the FTC noted in its summary: "The program for equal employment opportunity has not been effectively implemented throughout the agency."

In the same report, the Civil Service Commission emphasized:

> Much greater effort must be made to seek out minority group candidates for professional positions. The system of almost total reliance on walk-ins must be replaced with a program of aggressive search if the Federal Trade Commission is to be assured that it is getting its fair share of top quality minority group candidates.

There are currently five Negroes in the GS 9–18 grades for professional employees. One is a librarian, three are attorneys, and one is a textile investigator. According to a member of the Office of Personnel who is in a position to know about the FTC's recruiting effort, Chairman Dixon has effectually disobeyed this Civil Service Commission directive. According to this source, Chairman Dixon had made no apparent effort in recent years to encourage Negroes to join the FTC. As a result, no change in minority recruitment policies has taken place since 1965. In 1966 an attorney was going to be sent to Howard Law School to do special recruiting. Because of minor disturbances on the campus, he decided not to go. Since that attempt the Personnel Office has justified not visiting Howard by invoking the general rule that it does not send interviewers to any of the District of Columbia law schools. A major problem is that the FTC has no young black attorneys who can be sent to interview black law students. The problem would solve itself if the Commission were to follow the edict of the Civil Service Commission and make a vigorous effort to hire competent Negro lawyers. The final suggestions of the Civil Service Report were that the FTC should provide:

1. an intensive educational program to assure full understanding of the equal opportunity program by all personnel.

2. a positive recruiting program to utilize vacancies which are occurring, in the field in particular, to place qualified clerical and professional candidates in offices which have few or no minority group members on the rolls.

As of fall, 1968, three years after the report was issued, the FTC had acted on neither provision.

In "The Dim Light of Paul Rand Dixon," an article that appeared in *The Washingtonian*, October, 1968, Milton Viorst concludes:

Paul Rand Dixon's chief failure . . . seems to be that he's been with the Federal Trade Commission far too long. Dixon is so accustomed to doing what he's always done that he finds it difficult to conceive of doing anything very different. . . .

He simply lacks the clarity of conception necessary to

give the FTC broad new objectives, as well as the tenacity of spirit needed to build a staff equal to achieving them.

With this kind of leadership it is not surprising that a large number of the "old-timers" are considerably less than vigorous.[1] The Office of the General Counsel epitomizes this problem. Including the General Counsel, there are thirty-two attorneys in the office. Of these thirty-two, twenty-two hold a GS rank of 15 or higher, which carries a salary of $20,000 to $25,000, primarily because of their long tenure at the Commission. GS-15 is as high as one can go without getting into supergrades. Another five are GS-14's, three are GS-13's, one is a GS-11, and one is a GS-9. The progression, then, is like an upside-down pyramid.

The General Counsel, James McI. Henderson, a Johnson man from Texas, started his political career clerking for the late Senator Marvin Sheppard of Texas. In better days he occupied a number of significant governmental positions. Now, as General Counsel to the FTC, he is frequently absent from his office. In our two separate attempts to interview him, he was not there, and his embarrassed secretary could not say when he would be back or whether he was on extended leave, vacation, or what. At other times during the summer we tried to reach him by telephone at his office, with similar results.

---

[1] A reporter in the January 13, 1969, issue of *Newsweek* quoted one Commissioner as saying, "a lot of old-timers appointed by Dixon have lapsed into a state of lethargy," and added that "another agreed that there was a great deal of drinking on the job." We pinpointed the favorite spots for an office-hours snort at Stevie's, which is down the street from the FTC, and the Saxony, which is also nearby.

Most young attorneys at the Commission, and a few in high GS levels, are critical of the personnel in the General Counsel's Office. "It is the office of sinecures," one remarked. Another commented, "there is a lot of 'deadwood' on the fifth floor." (That floor houses—besides the entire Office of the General Counsel—Chairman Dixon's office, Commissioner MacIntyre's office, and the office of the Executive Director.)

Some of the men in the General Counsel's Office are desperately in need of face-saving. One of these is Charles Grandey. When two members of our task force went to interview Mr. Grandey in his office, they found him fast asleep on a couch with the sports section of *The Washington Post* covering his head. They woke him up, and he walked to his desk, where he propped his chin up with his hands on top of a pile of books. Asked what his work entailed, Mr. Grandey gave a very vague reply. Further inquiries with other FTC attorneys established that he really did very little, his chief occupation being to abstract cases pertinent to the Commission's work. His yearly salary is $22,695. He is officially listed in the Commission telephone book as Assistant General Counsel for Voluntary Compliance, along with the other assistant general counsels who head divisions. He is also listed on organization charts in the same manner, but in the confidential budget-control reports, he is simply placed along with the assistants *to* the General Counsel. And just exactly what the Division of Voluntary Compliance does is a mystery not solved even by the FTC's *Justification of Estimates of Appropriations for Fiscal Year* for 1968 and 1969, which are presented to Congress. In these tomes the Division of Voluntary Compliance mysteriously disappears and remains unjustified.[1]

The Office of the General Counsel with all its inefficiencies resulting from too many high-ranking staff attorneys is representative of the central office of the Commission. Of the 319 attorneys there (the field offices have 155), 34 per cent are GS-15's or higher, 22 per cent are GS-14's, 15 per cent are GS-13's, 6 per cent are GS-12's, 10 per cent are GS-11's, and 13 per cent are GS-9's.[2] These percentages do not include the Commissioners, the Executive Director, or the hearing examiners, all of whom are at the central office and hold supergrades above GS-15. In short, the FTC is suffering from a bad case of too many chiefs and too few Indians. A constant complaint heard from younger attorneys concerned interference from higher-ups with overlapping jurisdictions and "their desire to direct, not work."

Here, again, we find a situation that was vigorously brought to Chairman Dixon's attention by the 1965 Civil Service Report. In the "Summary Evaluation of the Report," the following points are made:

—A number of key positions have overlapping, duplicative, conflicting assignments of duties and responsibilities.
—Positions are assigned grade-influencing duties that are not being performed.
—Attorneys are not assigned work commensurate with their grade level.

[1] After this report was released, one young FTC attorney remarked: "Why single out that poor old guy? He's going to retire in a couple of years anyway." Rounded off, that will cost the taxpayers about $45,000.
[2] The GS-10 rank is not applicable to attorneys.

—The head of the agency is not meeting those responsibilities placed upon him by the Classification Act of 1949.

Bright Men Need Not Apply

According to the myth about hiring that the Federal Trade Commission encourages, it seeks out the best young attorneys and offers them appointments. Our confidential interviews told a different story. Young attorneys are accepted for various reasons. Some on the merits of their case—grades, extracurricular activities, and Law School Admission Test scores; but many more are accepted because the interviewers "liked" them, or because of old school ties, regional background, or a political endorsement.

The major hurdle for a graduating law student who wishes an appointment is the interview with the bureau chief or an assistant in the bureau he wishes to join. He must in addition fill out a formal application which asks for school, grades, academic honors, admission test scores, home state, and pertinent courses he might have taken in law school. But, according to all those involved in running the admission process, the interview makes or breaks the applicant. From 1958 to 1959 there was a "rating sheet for attorney applications." It used a point system that minimized the effect of the interview. The bureau chiefs, however, became very dissatisfied with this system, and it was discontinued.[1]

---

[1] Much to his credit, the Director of Personnel is again attempting to minimize the effect of the bureau chiefs by using mid-level attorneys instead of bureau chiefs for a number of the interviews. The bureau

The myth of a hunt for the best available legal talent has been dispelled by Chairman Dixon, who has been quoted as saying: "Given a choice between a really bright man, and one who is merely good, take the good man. He'll stay longer." [1]

Chairman Dixon's well-known prejudice against "Ivy League lawyers" is deeply rooted in Southern populist tradition, which is the background of the Commission's ruling clique.[2] As a result, graduates of prestigious law schools such as Harvard and Pennsylvania, which have very capable antitrust departments, have a poor chance of joining the FTC, compared with graduates of law schools like Kentucky and Tennessee. Eleven Harvard graduates from the classes of '67 and '68 applied to the FTC, and only four were offered appointments. From the University of Pennsylvania, only three of nine applicants were given offers, and from New York University only three of thirty-four applicants made it. However, from the University of Kentucky it was nine out of eleven and from Tennessee six out of sixteen. It is possible, of course, that individually the applicants from Southern schools were better than those from the North. But this

chiefs, of course, still have a veto over the offers made for their bureaus, but now it is more difficult for them to raise objections to particular applicants on the basis of an interview. However, a number of the higher-ups at the FTC have already objected to this innovation, and it will probably go the way of the rating sheet.

[1] *Advertising Age*, November 20, 1961, p. 113.

[2] The "Eastern conspiracy" of bankers and lawyers has played a prominent role in populist demonology. It is unfortunate that the present lethargy of the Commission has drained from its members the intense dislike of monopoly that is one of the good characteristics of Southern populism.

is not borne out by available data [1]—comparing, for example, applicants from the University of Kentucky, 82 per cent of whom were accepted, with those from New York University, with 9 per cent acceptances. Kentucky draws its law students from its immediate region, while N.Y.U. has a prestigious "national" law school, attracting students throughout the country. In 1967 and 1968 the graduating law students at Kentucky had, on the average, scored in the 42nd percentile on their Law School Admission Test. On the same tests, the N.Y.U. students had averaged in the 82nd percentile, almost twice as high. There seems little doubt that if a law student in the top 50 per cent of his class at N.Y.U. suddenly were transplanted to Kentucky, he would be in at least the top 25 per cent of his new class. The average Kentucky applicant to the FTC is indeed in the top 25 per cent of his class, while the average N.Y.U. applicant is in the top 50 per cent—against far stiffer competition. The distinction is lost on the FTC, which asks for but ignores Law School Admission scores, relying instead on interviews and undifferentiated grades. When in our report, we recommended that the FTC end its discrimination against the national law schools by devising a system that relates class standings with test scores, Chairman Dixon replied:

> The Nader group infers strongly that the hiring practices of the commission discriminates against "prestigious" law schools. Indirectly, I read in this charge that if a graduat-

[1] In Appendix, Sections 12–14, we chart applicants and job offers against region, Law School Admission-Test scores, and for the class of '68 an honors code number derived from class standing and extracurricular activities.

ing student did not attend one of these schools he is adjudged a second-class lawyer coming from a mediocre school. What arrogance!

The attitude of the bureau chiefs is such that they prefer new attorneys who will not underscore their elders' mediocrity or disturb the work patterns of their bureau. It is easy to eliminate the bright young fellows from national law schools by finding fault in interviews and, for a clincher, pointing to class standing. The perpetuation of mediocrity goes beyond a phobia of the East. Graduates of the University of Virginia Law School, one of the good national law schools, are treated as badly as graduates from good Eastern schools. Of thirteen Virginia graduates from the '67 and '68 classes who applied to the FTC, only two were accepted.

Our analysis of applicants and FTC hiring practices for 1967 and 1968 indicates that graduates from the South are accepted two to one over graduates from the North. The figure is three to one for offers to join one of the bureaus in the central Washington office. For Northerners 36 per cent are offered appointments in field offices; for Far Westerners, 72 per cent; for Mid-Westerners, 36 per cent. For political reasons, some Southern states have an advantage over other states. Tennessee has an acceptance rate of 52 per cent, Texas 53 per cent. New York and Massachusetts have 22 per cent and 31 per cent respectively. A high acceptance rate for Tennessee applicants is not remarkable considering Joe Evins's influence at the FTC and the fact that Chairman Dixon and Executive Director Wheelock, both from Tennessee, are the final authorities on offers granted. According to sources in the FTC close to the selection process, these two men have misused their powers by hiring attorneys who have not gone through the normal application process of submitting law-school grades and other pertinent data. School ties also affect an applicant's chances. For example, George Washington University, which is strongly represented on the FTC upper staff, and the University of Texas fare unusually well even for good law schools.

Section 13 of the Appendix demonstrates that no significant difference in legal aptitude and law-school standing exists between Northern and Southern applicants. Considering that more than twice as many Northerners as Southerners applied to the FTC, one could expect twice as many well-qualified Northerners applying to the Commission and, consequently, twice as many Northerners receiving offers of appointment. The LSAT scores for appointments offered indicate that less capable students are being accepted from inferior schools. Students offered appointments have a higher rank in class, but lower basic aptitude for law.

Within four years 80 per cent of the new lawyers leave the FTC. Their reasons vary from a chance at a better-paying job to complete detestation for the agency. We interviewed five young attorneys who had left or were about to leave. Three were working for law firms in Washington, one was at the Justice Department, and one was getting ready to leave. We spoke briefly with a sixth, but he subsequently balked at a full interview, fearing recriminations in the form of bad recommendations from the FTC. He, too, was in the process of leaving. All of these attorneys were unanimous in the opinion that the FTC was a discouraging place for a young attorney. Most had stayed for as long as they did only to finish their "graduate on-the-job training" in antitrust law and to qualify for good recommendations.

One lawyer who had been at the FTC in the late 1950's and early 1960's stated that the aggressive trial approach of Chairman Earl Kintner was ideal for young lawyers who wanted to take responsibility. He calculated that he had tried nineteen cases in his first two-and-a-half years because his boss liked nothing better than to shift his workload onto willing young attorneys. After those exciting first years, however, things slowed down under the Dixon regime and its voluntary-compliance approach. The younger lawyers "got pissed," he said, when the higher-ups started to let cases they had prepared for trial sit around for months without any action. This lawyer stated that he had once prepared a memorandum recommending complaint and that eighteen months later it had not left his boss's office.

Another lawyer who had been at the FTC during the same period said that there had been a lot of "esprit de corps" in his bureau (Restraint of Trade), but that it had diminished by 1963 because so few cases were being tried. He explained that the young trial lawyers love to fight big companies, but that the hierarchy at the FTC usually ends up going after the little guy at the request of Congressmen.

The Division of Discriminatory Practices, which enforces almost exclusively violations under the Robinson-

Patman Act,[1] provides a good example of the problem of young lawyers at the FTC. Before 1960, approximately seventy complaints under the Robinson-Patman Act were filed each year. Now, however, with a substantially larger number of attorneys working in the same field, only six or seven complaints are issued each year. Younger lawyers, eager to prove themselves, write memoranda recommending complaint on a large number of investigations, but these memoranda are reviewed successively by one of the elder attorneys in the division (there are eleven GS-15's among the thirty-nine attorneys in the division), by Peter Dias, a GS-15 who reviews all recommendations for complaint, and by the division chief, Frank Meyer. This results in months of inaction, petty changes, and misallocated attorney-hours, which in turn result in the small number of actual complaints. The young lawyers who issue the original memoranda cannot help being disappointed and discouraged. The division chief in this case has also underutilized and offended his younger staff. Often two attorneys are assigned to the same investigation, but neither is told that the other is duplicating his work. If an assiduous worker completes his assigned duties early and requests additional work, he is not given another investigation but is assigned to write a research paper on the Robinson-Patman Act. When finished, the paper is not disseminated to the entire staff, but curiously remains the personal and secret property of the division chief.

This pattern of discouragement is repeated in various

---

[1] Designed to prevent sellers from giving advantages to some buyers and not to all.

forms in other divisions. In the Division of Mergers, for example, an eager GS-9 incurred the wrath of his chief by protesting the minimal quantity of work he was given. Although he had been at the FTC for only two years, he decided to leave. His chief, angered by the ripples he had caused in an otherwise peaceful pond, punished him for his energy and ability by refusing to give a good recommendation. Only after transferring to another division did he manage to escape from the bonds of the Commission.

It is no wonder, then, that four out of every five new attorneys leave within four years.

An old hand at the Federal Trade Commission stated that there were two kinds of people among the lawyers that decided to make a career of the FTC:

1. the intelligent, idealistic public servants who also desire a certain degree of security, and

2. the not-so-smart lawyers who need the security of the FTC.

Most of the career men at the FTC fall into the second category.[1] We interviewed one of the few in the first category. He was a frustrated man, working under comparatively inept superiors, who was now doing his work more out of professional pride than idealism.

In the last analysis, the major problem at the FTC is motivational. The men who lead the Commission desire only to do the work they have always done in a manner that recalls Samuel Beckett's existential tragedy *Waiting*

---

[1] According to Robert Sherwood, Director of Personnel, one of the most important influences on the number of applications to the FTC is the state of the economy. More lawyers apply in hard times than in boom times, apparently because there is economic security in a government job.

for Godot. In the meantime, the young attorneys at the bottom languish for want of direction and remind themselves they are there for only a short while to receive a practical legal education.

Lawyers Are Not Enough

The FTC's large staff of lawyers also poses a problem of quite a different order—legal competence alone is often not enough for the job.

The Division of Food and Drug Advertising in the Bureau of Deceptive Practices is a good case in point. It is responsible, among other things, for detecting and preventing deception in drug-product advertising. Yet it is staffed entirely by lawyers and has no doctors or scientists to advise it, according to Dr. Barbara Moulton of the Division of Scientific Opinions (which only evaluates claims referred to it by the Division of Food and Drug Advertising, doing no monitoring on its own). It is then not surprising that the Division of Food and Drug Advertising operates at a low level of energy (six of twenty-one staff attorneys left between June, 1966, and June, 1968, according to the division chief, John W. Brookfield). It also does nothing at all to enforce the agency's laws on therapeutic devices (the statute includes "foods, drugs and devices").

Then there is the "odometer" case. For some thirty years the FTC knew that automobile odometers—which register mileage—were "fast," giving inflated figures. Automobile manufacturers and rent-a-car companies benefited. No one but the car owner lost. The FTC knew yet did nothing. The reason was that the FTC was duped over and over again by the excuse that the auto manufacturers put forth. Detroit stated that it *had* to make odometers register high because state highway officials demanded that it make *speed*ometers register high (to diminish actual driving speeds), and that the two were inseparably connected. As any mechanical engineer would have known, the odometer and speedometer are *not* connected. Since they work by different mechanisms —the odometer by gears, the speedometer by magnetic induction—it is perfectly feasible to adjust one without affecting the other.

Unfortunately, the FTC did not have any engineers on its staff, nor does it now. And now, as the complexity of consumer products increases, technical expertise is needed more than ever. Who on the FTC knows about the complex features of modern automobiles or their accessories? Who about household appliances and their qualities? Who about new construction materials and their properties? Who about electronic computers and their capabilities?

It is clear that with a debilitating disease, one's spirit, capabilities, and accomplishments are seriously affected. The question is, "is there time left to attempt a cure?"

THE CURES

IN THIS SECTION, which contains the findings and recommendations of the original version of our report, we shall try to sum up. We will address ourselves again to some of the most important issues raised and present them in brief sections. What is done with the material and how that is done will depend on a number of things—whether you as reader are a government official, whether our points have been convincing, whether you are concerned about change. Having published the report of our study, we cannot be content until you have joined us in some attempt at correcting the ills we describe.

Here, in the last third of the twentieth century, the awesome march of technology has given the American consumer modern advertising, with its powers to manipulate irrational forces in the human personality. Coupled with the pervasive impact of modern communications, it presents a challenge to the government to step in on behalf of the consumer, to protect and preserve the right

163

to "rational" choice. This is a complicated subject and little is known about it, but its importance grows daily. The mandate the Congress has given the Federal Trade Commission puts within the agency's province the question of whether sophisticated motivational-research advertising is a "deceptive" or "unfair" practice. This question should always be weighed in FTC deliberations. It should also soon become a subject of specific investigation and consideration.

The FTC's present methods of becoming aware of consumer problems are woefully inadequate. It relies almost exclusively on letters of complaint from the public to detect possible violations of its laws, yet it cannot obtain monetary satisfaction for injured individuals. As a result, there is little incentive to report deceptions to the Commission. Moreover, since many deceptive business practices are extremely subtle, victims may never know clearly that they have been deceived.

As a remedy, the Commission must begin to investigate consumer problems as such, making maximum use of its compulsory information-gathering powers. It should, for example, focus its attacks on specific and pressing problems by mobilizing efforts on a task-force scale, similar to the recent special project in Washington, D.C. It should hold related and frequent public hearings, publishing reports based on them, and it should pressure other government agencies—such as the Departments of Defense and Agriculture—to divulge information of interest to consumers.

The Commission's attorneys must make contact with

the people and the problems of the ghetto. Either through the roving task-force approach or through the establishment of storefront offices in ghetto areas, the FTC must become visible to disenfranchised America. Commissioners and staff members down to the lowest levels must establish contact with the burgeoning grass-roots self-help organizations forming in every large city. The FTC must defer its talks before trade associations, however pleasant, in favor of meetings with the poor and exploited, to set up two-way communication. It must establish field offices where they are needed and relocate those that are not, particularly the one in Oak Ridge, Tennessee. And it must make them into centers for aggressive investigations.

The FTC should consider requiring manufacturers and advertisers of major or potentially harmful products to file reports on their products containing data to substantiate claims made about them. This would shift the burden of proof to the businessman—as the Food and Drug Administration does in regulating new drugs.

Simultaneously, the Commission must beef up its public-complaint system, perhaps by passing legislation to let injured consumers sue for treble damages, using FTC cease and desist orders to establish a *prima facie* case. Massive and pointed consumer education is essential.

The FTC still fails to select only important cases for prosecution, exhausting its limited resources in handling trivial cases as it has for more than fifty years. Little can be recommended except that it finally begin to make decisions according to the criteria it claims to use (size of company, seriousness of deception, class and number of consumers affected). In practical terms, a good start would be to find a hard-hitting successor to the late Charles Sweeney, the Program Review Officer, whose position has been vacant since his death in 1968. The new Program Review Officer should have solid grounding in cost-benefit analysis and computer operation and should be provided with the thorough, honest, and intelligently shaped performance statistics that do not now exist.

The Commission fails woefully to enforce its laws properly in the context of its present powers. It relies much too heavily—nearly exclusively—on "voluntary," nonbinding enforcement tools. These cannot be expected to work at all unless they are backed up by stricter coercive measures, almost completely lacking now.

The agency also permits flagrant delays to sap its enforcement program. In the administrative handling of formal orders and in the investigative reports, the Commission fails to press forward with dispatch. This means toothless enforcement activity and long periods of inaction on the most pressing problems.

Finally, the FTC fails to perceive and take advantage of the enforcement potential of its most extensive authority—the power to require disclosure of information and publish it in the public interest.

To improve its enforcement, the Commission must begin by jettisoning its excessive reliance on voluntary methods. Where voluntary means *are* used, the FTC must check compliance more carefully and enforce it more stringently. Available coercive methods must get greater emphasis. At present, these powerful tools are almost entirely unused. The Commission must institute more frequent use of civil penalties as well as suits for preliminary injunctions and criminal penalties under the Flammable Fabrics Act and the food and drug provisions of the FTC Act.

The Commission must begin a program of periodic compliance checks on the entire number of outstanding cease and desist orders and begin to punish noncompliers harshly.

It must rout delays by marshaling sufficient legal and monetary resources to prosecute cases effectively and also by enjoining practices on which action is pending. Every matter taken up should be brought to a prompt and clean conclusion; never should announced investigations be allowed to vanish without a murmur.

Finally, the FTC must recognize that the threat of prompt, effective, and widespread publicity about objectionable corporate behavior is an enforcement tool of wide potential. We have seen that when some action is taken, large corporations are remarkably thin-skinned.

The Commission has not vigorously pressed for more statutory authority at large or in specific problem areas. In general, it needs the authority to seek preliminary injunctions and criminal penalties in cases involving Section 5 of the FTC Act. It should also seek changes in the act's language on jurisdiction to make clear its power in intrastate matters. In areas of specific problems the Commission should seek enforcement tools as effective as the power the Securities and Exchange Commission has for stopping stockbrokers from trading and the Food and Drug Administration has for seizing drugs in condemnation proceedings.

On a different plane, the FTC should begin to lobby vigorously for the passage of "baby FTC Acts" by individual states in order to increase law enforcement for consumer protection.

In pushing for all this necessary new legislation, the Commission should be prepared to use its publicity and informational powers to mobilize maximum support among consumers. That is why an ongoing educational program is essential. A few booklets or news releases will never be enough. The Commission must not fail to press for the necessary appropriations and manpower to carry out its proper role. An increase eight to nine times the present appropriation would be a minimum initial target.

The FTC's fetish of secrecy masks from public view much of its regulation of business, preventing evaluation of its performance as well as of business practices involved. Solutions to this problem must be sought on all levels. The agency's policies on "confidential" classifications should conform to the requirements of the Freedom of Information Act. Public logs should be kept of all conferences between businessmen and the Commission's staff in order to minimize behind-the-scenes whitewashing of agency reports and unwholesome coziness between lawyers for private interests and agency staff members.

Public information must be made truly public by

general publication and dissemination; news releases must be made more concrete and informative. It would not be enough merely to call for increased numbers of reports to the public.

In cases of decisions not to take action, the FTC should publish its reasons rather than quietly shelving inquiries of potential importance.

Briefly, the FTC must change its philosophy, recognizing that citizens have as much right to important information as members of Congress and officers of large corporations.

There is little doubt where the leadership of the Federal Trade Commission resides—it is with Chairman Paul Rand Dixon. Professor Kenneth C. Davis, after surveying the regulatory agencies in person, observed that no other regulatory agency has witnessed such a concentration of *de jure* and *de facto* authority and power as that possessed by Chairman Dixon.

With greater centralization of agency power and authority go commensurately higher levels of responsibility. As the tenure of Mr. Dixon's chairmanship lengthens, more and more of the Commission's problems and defaults are attributable to his failures of leadership and not to the legacy of his predecessors. Unlike his predecessors, Mr. Dixon could have benefited from the recent upsurge in the consumer movement, with a growing constituency at many levels of society, from community organizations in the slums to Congress. Not only has he failed to recognize an ally in the growing concern for the consumer, but he has even chosen to view it skeptically and with no little disdain. While even the White House has passed him by in delineating new consumer-protection horizons, Mr. Dixon has trundled along and institutionalized mediocrity, rationalized a theory of endemic inaction, delay, and secrecy, and transformed the agency into the Government's Better Business Bureau. He has managed the not inconsiderable feat of turning the Federal Trade Commission into a patterned and intricate deceptive practice unto itself.

Such accomplishments could not be mismanaged without lieutenants. One of Mr. Dixon's undoubted skills is his alacrity in filling the Commission with his cronies. Besides its obvious faults, cronyism—especially when it comes from the boss—destroys internal criticism. This is not the time to evaluate bureau chiefs and other leading staff members, case by case. But it is highly appropriate to mention that alcoholism, spectacular lassitude, and office absenteeism, incompetence by the most modest standards, and a lack of commitment to the regulatory mission are rampant at these staff levels. They are well known to the Chairman, who somehow has found that they add to the congenial environment and unquestioned loyalties that surround his office. Even high officials of the Commission, who despair and depict in detail these staff liabilities, shy away from further action out of deference to the Chairman's power. Thus, the FTC is witness to a phenomenon of government that can be described at best as sinecures and at worst as $27,000-a-year welfare cases. Thus, at the higher staff levels, where policy direction, courage, and new ideas should proliferate, unproductive overhead and featherbedding prevail. They are major demoralizing influences that filter down to the fledgling FTC recruit, who soon realizes that life's potential is better tapped elsewhere.

The public arena for the FTC to flex its consumer-protection muscle has been growing larger with every passing month—such is the ambience that has flourished in recent years. Yet the Chairman has chosen to dance on the head of a pin and use its perch as his pretext for not doing the job. Most of the Commission's weaknesses and misdirection can be laid at the doorstep of the Chairman as the primary "responsable." [1] In the dim light of his record since 1961 and in view of his rigid and complacent official outlook, Mr. Dixon's chief and perhaps only contribution to the Commission's improvement would be to resign from the agency that he has so degraded and ossified. While we are aware of the political realities of such a suggestion, we offer it believing that his resignation would indicate to the American consumer, who has been deceived, defrauded, and ignored for profit by corporations large and small, that the FTC was finally prepared to protect his interest as demanded by law.

The new Chairman should undertake the formidable task of uprooting the political and regional cronyism that has for years prevented the FTC from achieving its mandate to defend the hapless consumer. The present bureau chiefs must be judged not on the strength of political friends, but for abilities and motivations. Those who do not measure up must be replaced without regard for seniority. Concurrently, junior attorneys must be granted

---

[1] Accountable official.

easy access to the Commissioners so that the normal channels of communication do not stifle innovation and vigorous action.

To obtain the best available legal talent, the FTC must change its hiring system. It can eliminate its institution-alized discrimination against the country's top law schools by a sophisticated system relating class standings with aptitude scores to grade various law schools. In addition, the Commission should consider evaluations of antitrust and consumer-law programs. Middle-grade at-torneys from at least below the division-chief level should conduct all interviews and take an active role in the acceptance process. This will prevent the current major problem—an upper management out of touch with the times that seeks its own image and perpetuates out-moded values. If gradual change is not built into our institutions, violent change will inevitably result.

The FTC should hire a limited number of full-time engineers, doctors, and product experts to supply con-tinual advice to attorneys investigating the complex items that characterize modern society. The Commission should do this even if it has to reduce the number of its lawyers.

At a minimum, the FTC must react to the mild criti-cisms of the Civil Service Commission, which have been publicly disclosed for the first time in this report. Chair-man Dixon has completely ignored the mandatory pro-visions of the Civil Service Commission 1965 Report. He

has not instituted computer education for his staff. He
has not aggressively sought attorneys from minority
groups. And he has increased, not decreased, the number
of high-level attorneys whose jobs do not justify their
civil-service ranks.

We have found that the Federal Trade Commission's
performance of its regulatory duties has been shockingly
poor. But because of the Commission's mask of secrecy,
what we discovered is only the visible fraction of what is
probably an iceberg of incompetence and mismanagement.

The Federal Trade Commission is much more open to
scrutiny by its Congressional watchdog committees than
by mere citizens. These committees—the Senate Commerce Committee and the House Interstate and Foreign
Commerce Committee—should undertake a full-scale
study of the FTC's consumer-protection activities. Such
an investigation should determine what can be done to
reorient the agency toward its proper role—protector of
the American consumer—and it should make future deviations from that role impossible.

VII

THE
AFTERMATH

When the Report Was Released

WE RELEASED OUR REPORT on January 6, 1969. It received a great deal of attention from the news media and was the subject of numerous editorials and magazine features. Administrative agencies, Congressional committees, law firms, advertising agencies, and trade associations have requested copies.

Several days after its release, Chairman Dixon issued his reply. It is reproduced in full below, followed by our rebuttal.

There has been much activity behind the scenes. Several officials have expressed interest in formal hearings. Meanwhile, there is a desperate struggle for the chairmanship of the Commission underway between Mr. Dixon and several of the other Commissioners. (President Nixon can choose a new Commission Chairman, but not new Commissioners until their terms expire or they resign.) Mr. Dixon feels his chief threat comes from the Commission's only Republican, Mary Jones. He is hoping to turn our criticism that he has been too much pro-business into an appealing feature for the benefit of an administration he sees as pro-business. Commissioner Jones, however, is not likely to be outflanked. *Women's Wear Daily* has reported that she is "taking unusual steps to advance her campaign: Asking retailer interests to get behind her candidacy and put in a good word with the Nixon Administration. . . . Recently, Miss Jones reversed herself and voted a tie breaking 'yes' on the Broadway-Hale–Neiman-Marcus merger deal."

The Chairman has circulated a memo to his staff urging, in the light of our report, that all employees be at work on time, leave only at quitting time, not drink on the job, and cover up any lunch imbibing with breath mints. It is also said that he has absolutely forbidden any discussion of the report and that anyone caught with a copy in his possession would soon be without a job.

The visceral reactions of the agency are quite predictable and illustrate the close tie between "personality" and job behavior. Chairman Dixon characterized the members of our project as "smart-aleck pricks" and "zealots" who would plant seeds of anarchism. According to the Chairman, we seek nothing but destruction and are out to "undermine" the agency. Ironically, the report itself predicted the Chairman's response with some accuracy: "He relishes describing them [consumer-protection groups] as wild-eyed zealots threatening the values of federalism and free enterprise. Meanwhile, he sees himself as the chief bulwark against their conspiracy for government control and tyranny." His response is characteristic, supporting, better than we could have asked, our descriptions of his philosophy. For not only was our project labeled anarchistic, but somehow we would also seek to make the agency too *strong* as well, thus imposing a "big brother" on America.

The reactions of the upper staff deserve comment. Generally, the project members are associated in their minds with everything they consider undesirable. Thus, Harvard and Yale are tossed together with long hair, drugs, homosexuality, hippies, crime, and riots into one curious and undifferentiated whole. A typical private comment from a member of the upper staff was "What do you expect from people behind all those city riots?"

We welcome critical discussion of our analysis. As yet, no one, including members of the Washington press corps, has effectively challenged a single substantive finding or conclusion of the report. Chairman Dixon, after directing his staff to pick the report apart, has produced instead of a constructive critique only the wild rhetoric that we now quote in full.

Statement of Chairman Paul Rand Dixon

The protection of the consuming public of the United States from fraud and deception is vital to free enterprise and the public interest. I believe strongly in that principle. Most of my adult and professional life, both at the Federal Trade Commission and as a member of the staff of the United States Senate, has been devoted to the study and elimination of trade and consumer abuses.

When I was made Chairman of the Federal Trade Commission in 1961, I found the staff of the Commission to consist of approximately the same number of personnel that comprised the staff in 1938, the year that I joined the Federal Trade Commission as a $2,000 P-1 attorney. Today the Commission has a staff of less than 1,200 members, including professional and clerical personnel. Our mandate from Congress is the widest and most inclusive of all of the independent regulatory bodies. We need the best advice and techniques available to carry out this broad mandate from Congress.

On June 17, 1968, Ralph Nader called on me at my office and informed me that a group of students and recent law school graduates wished to study the activities of the Commission. I welcomed the idea. After some discussion, I informed Mr. Nader that I had no objection to members of the staff being contacted and interviewed so long as it was done on a reasonable basis and that I had no objection to furnishing the group information in our files that was in the public domain. I hoped, and based on what I was told I had every reason to believe, that the result would be a serious, intelligent and impartial survey resulting in informed, conclusive suggestions for improvement. Instead, the study resulted in a hysterical, anti-business diatribe and a scurrilous, untruthful attack on the career personnel of the Commission and an arrogant demand for my resignation. This report emanates from a group with a self-granted license to criticize a respected government agency by the use of a type of invective and "smear technique" that newspapermen inform me is unusual even for Washington.

This Nader group chose the Federal Trade Commission as its target for its 1968 summer vacation "smear" project. As stated in the comment in *The Wall Street Journal* of July 10, 1968, on page 14, if this group is successful in undermining the Federal Trade Commission this year, then other groups of students may make similar raids on other agencies in the future. Mr. Nader is so quoted in this article as follows:

> The crusader has recruited five other students from leading universities, including William Howard Taft IV, great grandson of the Republican president, mainly to investigate what Mr. Nader terms the failure of the Federal Trade Commission to move boldly enough against deceptive business practices. "If this works, man, next summer, more students, more agencies . . ." Mr. Nader vows.

The feel of destructive power gained from vicious attacks is self-stimulating.

On the afternoon of January 2, 1969, I began to receive phone calls from the press and other media requesting my comments on the "Nader report," which obviously had been distributed to them. By letter of the same date, I was requested by the Public Broadcast Laboratory to appear on a half-hour program the night of Sunday, January 5, to reply to the statements in the report. I informed all requesting parties that I had not received a copy of the report and was unable to comment on it until I had been afforded the opportunity of at least reading it. Later that afternoon, I was called by Mr. John Schulz, who stated that a copy of the report had been mailed to me that day and that I should receive it soon.

I made it a point to watch the half-hour program by the Public Broadcast Laboratory, which appeared on TV station WETA at 9:30 P.M. on Sunday night, January 5. At one point the producer saw fit to dub in a previously taped interview with me, which made it appear that I was a part of the program dealing with the report itself. This was not true. At the time of this program I had not as yet even seen the report. When I reached my office on January 6, the promised report had not arrived and as of today, January 7, it still has not arrived. The copy on the basis of which I am now commenting was borrowed for me by the Commission's Information Officer from a member of the news media.

As I see it, ordinary courtesy would require the authors of such a document as this to provide me and the other members of the Commission with a copy of it before releasing it to the press. Since this was not done, I can only conclude that the preparation of this report was not the result of a serious, unbiased study of a group seeking to aid this agency in the performance of its public responsibilities, but was, on the other hand, a deliberate effort to undermine it.

Let's turn to the report itself. Laying aside the monotonous accusatory adverbs and adjectives in the critique, the primary difference between the fundamental position of the Nader group and that of myself is that I believe that the American businessman is basically honest and they believe he is basically dishonest, trying consistently to defraud the American consumer. The group contends that American business, particularly the larger corporations selling directly or indirectly to consumers and using extensive advertising, are engaged in what are, or should be, criminal activities and that the officers of these corporations should be sentenced to terms in federal penitentiaries. On page 68 of the critique, for example, it is stated: "It is particularly important to apply criminal sanctions to dishonest corporate behavior, for it is far more damaging in contemporary America than all the depredations of street crime." In other words, corporation executives are engaged in much more reprehensible conduct than rapists, robbers, muggers, etc. In light of this extreme anti-business bias of these young zealots, it is not surprising that the equitable and reasonable enforcement policies of the Commission would be so enthusiastically and unjustifiably criticized.

Shortly after I became Chairman of the Federal Trade Commission, the Commission turned from its general policy of emphasizing case-by-case adjudication to one seeking broader compliance with the law through new procedures. Experience had taught me that the case-by-case approach standing alone was not appropriate in the 1960's. The problems of regulatory lag and trial by convenience had been noted by the Landis Report and referred to by President Kennedy in his State of the Union message shortly after he assumed office.

The Commission's new procedures contemplated the broad use of guidelines, statements, trade regulation rules and advisory opinions. Also, where warranted, the Commission began to accept assurances of voluntary compliance under the many statutes which it administers. The Commission turned to these new procedures with a belief that by their use justice could be administered more equitably by government. This technique has proved successful. With its limited personnel, the Commission realized that it had to reserve its litigation procedures for use against that small percentage of businessmen in the business community that refused to follow advice.

Running throughout the Nader group report is the repeated reference to the failure of this program and that the Commission is in error in believing that any worthwhile compliance with its laws can result from any procedure other than formal adjudicative trials. In other words, the promise of a businessman cannot be trusted. In a people's government no law is any better than the will of the people to abide by it. I have great faith in the honest businessman of America. I do not think he loves his country any less than do these young zealots.

On pages 58 and 59 of the report, reference is made to the fact that Ralph Nader acquired a copy of a report dealing with automobile warranties and made it public. It is charged that the report was deliberately suppressed. On page 59, the following appears:

> The real reason for the proposed plan for suppression lay in the contents of the report, which was highly critical of GM, Ford and Chrysler. Whether release would have eventually occurred is academic now, but there is little doubt based upon our interviews that Chairman Dixon was determined to suppress the report at least until after the election to avoid alienating Henry Ford II and other business interests who were contributing heavily to Hubert Humphrey's campaign.

This is a false charge and a blatant lie. Such unfounded charges as this would appear to me to be beneath the dignity of Ralph Nader. I think it is high time that the press confront Mr. Nader with this statement and inquire expressly if he agrees with it. If he does, I think somebody in America had better start worrying about Mr. Nader.

The Nader group vigorously contend that because many of the key staff members of the Commission were born in small communities they cannot understand or appreciate the consumer problems of urban America and, therefore, should be replaced. This novel qualification test for those public officials having responsibility for considering the problems of urban America would have disqualified most of the Presidents of the United States, the vast majority of the Members of Congress and at least some of the Justices of the Supreme Court. The suggestion springs both from ignorance and arrogance. In addition, the students overlooked the fact that practically all of these key members of our staff, as well as the Chairman, have been living in urban metropolitan Washington, D.C., since before the students were born.

Nothing galls me more than that section of the Nader group report which accuses me of hiring only high-ranking law students from "mediocre" law schools. For a number of years I have sent to the Deans of all the major law schools and most, if not all, accredited law schools throughout the United States, letters requesting them to encourage their graduating seniors to apply for employment at the Federal Trade Commission. I am proud to say that my efforts in soliciting the many Deans have proved quite successful. The Federal Trade Commission has always had many more applicants than positions available. With rare exception, offers of employment have been made to applicants who graduated in the upper 50% of their class or had other outstanding attributes that made them attractive to the Federal Trade Commission. I have consistently believed any federal establishment is a better agency when its staff membership comes from various sections of the country. The Nader group infers strongly that the hiring practices of the Commission discriminates against "prestigious" law schools. Indirectly, I read in this charge that if a graduating student did not attend one of these schools he is adjudged a second-class lawyer coming from a mediocre school. What arrogance!

The lowest of all blows in the report is the charge on page 114 that "The FTC has not been averse to hiring Negroes, but 'only in their place,' i.e. the lowest GS 1–4 positions." Here are the facts. Since assuming my office as Chairman, I have made a positive effort to attract and hire qualified Negroes for attorney positions and other professional positions. In 1961, I found that there was not one Negro lawyer on the Commission staff. Starting in 1961, I was able, as a result of an internship program at the Commission, to persuade the top-ranking law student at Howard University to accept an appointment as a staff member. Since that time, by the adoption of more aggressive recruitment measurements, I have been able to persuade nine other Negroes to join the staff as attorneys. Five are still so employed. (The Nader report states that the Commission has only three Negro lawyers.) Many other Negroes have been offered appointments, but have generally declined the offers for the stated reason that they had offers which involved working in the civil rights area.

In short, contrary to allegations made in the report, the Federal Trade Commission has been engaged in a continuing, positive effort to recruit high quality personnel, including minority group candidates. To those involved in developing and promoting this effort, it is disheartening to read the unfounded allegations made in the Nader group report. The report paints a completely false picture of the Federal Trade Commission's efforts and accomplishments in the areas of recruitment and equal opportunity. This false picture will do untold damage to the Commission's continuing effort in this regard. What a shame to be faced with this problem at this time in the life of America.

The Nader group report contains unfounded false accusations with respect to political influences at the Federal Trade Commission. For instance, the report says that of the nearly 500 attorneys on the staff of the Commission that only about 40 are Republicans. Since assuming office on March 21, 1961, I have borne the responsibility of hiring new attorneys on the Commission's staff. The great majority of the attorneys that have been hired over the period 1961 to date have been graduating seniors from law schools. Under no condition and at no time was anyone connected with this program authorized to inquire into the party affiliation of an applicant. How the Nader group arrives at this mystical figure of 40 Republicans, I do not know. There is nothing in the Federal Trade Commission records to reveal it. It appears to me that this is another charge grossly unfounded.

Throughout the report reference is made to a report of the Civil Service Commission dated June 1965. This report was made by the Civil Service Commission as a part of its regular program of inspecting personnel management in Federal agencies and is considered a part of the internal housekeeping process in the Federal government. Repeatedly in referring to this report, the Nader group charges that the recommendations in the report have been ignored. However, this is absolutely not true. Contrary to the false statements respecting action recommended by the Civil Service Commission, I, in fact, adopted virtually all of the recommendations.

How any group could profess or claim to have made an empirical study of the activities of the Federal Trade Commission and make no mention of at least a single accomplishment by the Commission is beyond me. I shall mention a few.

The Commission's issuance of a Trade Regulation Rule in regard to disclosures of health hazards of cigarette smoking stimulated the enactment of the *Federal Cigarette Labeling and Advertising Act*, P.L. 89–92.

The Commission's proposal to issue guides relating to retail installment selling in the District of Columbia and in interstate commerce, and testimony furnished by the Commission with respect to abuses in credit selling, contributed in large measure to enactment of the *Consumer Credit Protection Act*, sometimes known as the *Truth-in-Lending Act*, P.L. 90–321.

The Commission played a major role in bringing about

an enactment of the *Amendments to the Flammable Fabrics Act,* P.L. 90–189, to give the public more adequate protection against flammability of household fabrics.

The Commission was a prime mover in proposing the bill known as the *Deceptive Sales Act of 1968,* S. 3065, which passed the Senate in July 1968. This bill would enable the Commission to obtain a temporary injunction in a United States District Court to halt violations affecting the consumer, pending completion of the administrative proceedings. In 1962, President Kennedy had endorsed passage of legislation which would have permitted the Commission on a proper showing of irreparable harm and injury to have sought temporary injunctions in a United States District Court on all facets of its work.

In consultation with Senator Magnuson, the Commission conducted a pilot project in the District of Columbia to identify the types of deceptive and unfair trade practices that might be preying upon poor people. The results were published in the June 1968 *Report on District of Columbia Consumer Protection Program.* To characterize this effort on the Commission's part as "so small and half-hearted that it could be called a showcase for publicity purposes" is both vain and unrealistic. This very effort at one point required approximately one-third of the appropriations available to the total Deceptive Practices program.

In making this study, the Commission was fully aware that it had many responsibilities for actions in the District of Columbia. It was believed then, and it still is my belief, that the lessons learned from this study are applicable to the various states of the nation which have the responsibility for unfair and deceptive acts occurring in "intrastate" commerce. Even the Nader group recognized the need for changes in the jurisdiction of the Commission if the Commission is to create offices in Detroit and Philadelphia and other cities to assume dual responsibility with the States.

The Commission's economic study of *Installment Credit and Retail Sales Practices of District of Columbia Retailers*, published in 1968, illuminated the problems of retailing in low-income areas. This study gave great impetus to the need for the *Truth-in-Packaging* legislation.

The Commission's economic studies on *Milk and Bread Prices* in 1966, the *Baking Industry* in 1967, and *Games of Chance in Supermarket and Gasoline Retailing* in 1969, as well as earlier reports on *Organization and Competition in Food Retailing*, *The Structure of Food Manufacturing*, and *Anticompetitive Practices in Gasoline Marketing*, contribute to the general fund of knowledge needed by the Commission, the Congress and interested members of the public in carrying forward and developing an effective trade regulatory program.

The *Economic Report on Webb-Pomerene Associations* in 1967, will undoubtedly have a significant effect on foreign trade policy.

The report on *Cents-Off Promotions in the Coffee Industry* in 1966, serves as a basis for consideration of regulations which may be issued under the "cents-off" provisions of the *Fair Packaging and Labeling Act*.

The staff report on *Automobile Warranties* forms the basis for public hearings soon to be held wherein the Commission will be determining the need, if any, for a trade regulation rule in this area.

I have felt compelled to mention these few actions on the part of the Commission because I think the public is entitled to know the important role the Commission has played and is playing in the area of consumer protection.

Most of us are producers and sell in some manner our talents and efforts, and all of us are consumers. The one should be in balance with the other. The Commission's role is to guide and advise the producer and, if necessary, to curb deception and to aid in informing the consumer.

I intend to remain at the Commission, consistently seeking better ideas and better techniques and increased efficiency in the operation of the Commission in fulfilling its very important role in protecting the consumer public. I intend to use my efforts to prevent, if I can, the extreme anti-business bias as exemplified by the views of these energetic, but misguided, students from poisoning the operation of the Federal Trade Commission to which I have given so much of my life.

January 9, 1969

A Reply to Chairman Dixon

On January 9, 1969, Chairman Paul Rand Dixon of the Federal Trade Commission issued an eight-page State-

ment which purported to answer criticisms of his and the
agency's performance contained in a 185-page Critique
entitled *The Consumer and the Federal Trade Commission* [hereinafter "Critique"] which had been made public the previous week. The Chairman's Statement is
erroneous in many particulars; this Reply will be devoted
to a dispassionate analysis of that Statement and an
attempt to correct its errors.

General Comments

Before discussing specific criticisms in the Statement,
the authors believe that it is important to deal with two
larger matters. In the first place, although the Statement
repeatedly uses emotion-laden rhetoric to charge that the
Critique is filled with "hysterical . . . untruthful" attacks and "unfounded false accusations," it singles out
only eight of those "accusations" to challenge in detail.
In other words, it passes in silence over scores of empiri-
cally based detailed criticisms contained in the Critique.
Thus, in addition to the fact that—as subsequent discussion will demonstrate—each of the eight points challenged by Mr. Dixon is in fact valid and well-founded,
the overwhelming conclusion to be drawn from the
Chairman's Statement is that he admits by implication
the validity of the great bulk of other closely documented
findings and criticisms contained in the Critique.

The second broad-scale matter which must be dis-
posed of is the Statement's characterization of the
motives and attitudes of Mr. Ralph Nader and of the
authors of the Critique. It first suggests that in investi-

gating the FTC they were motivated by a vicious desire to wield destructive power and that the Critique is in reality an effort to "undermine" the Federal Trade Commission. This is untrue, as a cursory reading of the Critique's "Recommendations" section will demonstrate. In fact, it seems a bit ironic for the authors to be accused of destructive motives when their concern, unlike that of some of their contemporaries, is to bring about improvement of an existing institution through normal channels and procedures.

More significant, the Chairman accuses the authors of the Critique of believing that "the American businessman is basically dishonest" while he believes "that the American businessman is basically honest." To support the charge of anti-business attitudes, the Statement continues

The group [authors] contends that American business, particularly the larger corporations . . . are engaged in what are, or should be, criminal activities and that the officers of these corporations should be sentenced to terms in federal penitentiaries. On page 68 of the Critique, for example, it is stated: "It is particularly important to apply criminal sanctions to dishonest corporate behavior, for it is far more damaging in contemporary America than all the depredations of street crime."

The authors respectfully submit that they are not infected with an "anti-business bias." In the passage quoted from it, the Critique was engaged in a rational evaluation of the social costs of certain unethical business practices, and the quoted statement is objectively accurate: in economic terms, the damage done by fraud and related economic practices is many times that caused by "violent" street crimes such as robbery and burglary. To demonstrate this unexceptionable fact it suffices to cite a few well-known statistics.[1] For example, the total value of property taken from individuals by robbery in the United States in 1968 is estimated at less than $55 million, whereas detectable business frauds netted in excess of one *billion* dollars in the same year.[2]

The serious social costs of various economic practices have frequently led legislatures to declare them "crimes" —in fact "criminal" provisions are *already* found in most of the statutes enforced by the FTC. In view of this, the Critique's recommendations—that the Commission begin to make substantial use of its existing criminal powers and seek such powers in limited new areas—are not novel[3] suggestions of violently anti-business "zealots" but rather examples of responsible administrative and legislative recommendations.

In this connection, it is fitting to reiterate a specific

---

[1] Admittedly this purely economic analysis does not take into account psychic and physical harms associated with, for example, robbery and rape. Even these harms, however, are prevalent in "economic practices" of the kind discussed above: flammable fabrics burn, cigarettes damage health, faultily designed autos maim and kill, home-improvement frauds drive the poor to despair and starvation; pollution threatens health and recreation, etc.

[2] Estimate of Charles Sweeney, deceased, former Program Officer of FTC, July, 1968. See also *Subcomm. on Frauds and Misrepresentations Affecting the Elderly*, 89th Cong., 1st Sess., Report, p. 8 (1965).

[3] The Statement's characterization of these proposals as contentions that "officers of . . . corporations should be sentenced to terms in federal penitentiaries" is hardly accurate. Any implication that such suggestions are something new is further belied by experience under the antitrust laws, which have "criminal" provisions.

criticism of the Chairman's attitude toward his duties made in the Critique. This attitude (of uncritical solicitude for businessmen) is overly naïve and simplistic and therefore inappropriate for a man in Mr. Dixon's position. By approaching the problem of business regulation with the statement that "the American businessman is basically honest," Mr. Dixon fails to come to grips with the complex and varied consumer-protection problems involved in the American economy and in the practices of its various business entities, all of which are discussed at length in the Critique; such problems seem entirely absent from the Chairman's view.

Even in his terms, the Chairman's view is erroneous. Surely he must believe that at least some businessmen engage some of the time in some practices which violate laws administered by his agency. If he does not believe this, Chairman Dixon should at least *assume* it for purposes of his job as a government regulator of industry; otherwise, he is simply not fulfilling his responsibilities as a member of the Federal Trade Commission either to business or to the consuming public.

Specific Comments

The remainder of this Reply will deal *seriatim* with the specific matters discussed in the Statement. Many of these matters are relatively petty and seem to be designed primarily to divert attention from the substantial criticisms and recommendations contained in the Critique. In this Reply no effort will be made to reiterate the prescriptions contained in that document.

The Late Arrival of the Chairman's Copy

In the Statement, Mr. Dixon complains that he did not receive a copy of the Critique until long after it had been made available to the press, although he admits receiving a phone call informing him that a copy had been mailed to him. That phone call was accurate: a copy was mailed to Mr. Dixon two full days *before* the press-release date set for the Critique (Sunday evening, January 5, 1969). It was thought that the Chairman would thus receive a copy in plenty of time to comment on it. The authors are sorry that they thus misjudged the efficiency of the United States Post Office's intra-city delivery service.

In addition, only a limited number of copies of the Critique were made available to reporters directly, and this was only to those reporters who had to meet weekly or daily closing deadlines for their publications (*Business Week, Newsweek,* for example, and various newspapers). The normal means of dissemination was and is by mail —the means used to transmit a copy to the Chairman.

Public Broadcast Laboratory Program

The Statement complains that the PBL program on the Critique, Sunday night, January 5, 1969, contained some misleading footage of a filmed interview with Chairman Dixon. Although this has nothing to do with the Critique, it should be pointed out for the benefit of those who did not see the program that the filmed interview with Chairman Dixon is clearly identified as having been carried out two months prior to the issuance of the Critique. It should also be noted that in that interview Mr. Dixon was responding to a "preview" of the Critique contained in a Statement read at the FTC's consumer-protection hearings of November, 1968, by Professor John Schulz, one of the Critique's three authors.

The "New" Approach to Regulation

In the Chairman's Statement there appears a brief, conclusory description of the supposed advantages of the FTC's recent shift to extensive use of "voluntary" means of enforcement. The many pages of theoretical and empirical objections raised in the Critique to the FTC's near-*exclusive* reliance on such enforcement tools are dismissed by the accusation that the authors of the Critique seem to believe that

> the promise of a businessman cannot be trusted. In a people's government no law is any better than the will of the people to abide by it. I have great faith in the honest businessman of America. I do not think he loves his country any less than do these young zealots.

Some of this rhetoric is a continuation of the charge of anti-business bias. Some exhibits again simplistic vision on the part of the Chairman (one suspects that the use of the singular—"the honest businessman"—may not be meant metaphorically). The first full sentence reflects excessive lack of understanding of the nature and function of law as deterrent. Thus, the Chairman seems unaware that criminal sanctions are more effective deterrents than others, certainly much more effective than no sanction at all ("assurances of voluntary compliance," discussed on p. 4 of the Statement, involve *no* sanction). More important, he seems not to realize that repeated and successful flouting of laws administered by the FTC is not conducive to maintenance of a "will of the people to abide by" those laws. Prohibition was a case in point.

Political Suppression of the Auto Warranty Report

The Statement takes issue with the Critique's allegation that political pressures involving the 1968 presidential campaign account for the long suppression of the FTC's auto warranty report. This information was made available to the authors of the Critique by a highly reliable source who is one of the Chairman's closest associates. We vouch for its accuracy.

Background of Key Staff Men

The Statement belittles the Critique's criticism of the fact that many top staff men at the FTC "were born in small communities." In so doing, it misrepresents the criticisms actually contained in the Critique on this point in two ways. First, it fails to do justice to the multiple strands of evidence on which the criticism is based: in the Critique, the fact of uniform small-town background does not stand alone; it is tied in with a description of unsophisticated attitudes expressed by these top staff men in interviews with the investigators of the project and with data on their political affiliations and favors.

Second, the Statement fails to mention that the precise criticism contained in the Critique referred as much to regional as to small-town domination of the FTC. As the Critique pointed out, *all* [1] key staff men in the bureaus relevant to the study came from *Southern* towns which also happen to be small. This thoroughgoing regional bias in top spots belies the Chairman's self-serving assertion that he has "consistently believed any federal establishment is a better agency when its staff membership comes from various sections of the country."

The Statement charges in addition that the Critique overlooked the fact that all the top staff men have long lived in "urban metropolitan Washington" and that they are therefore familiar with ghetto consumer problems. This formulation misrepresents the facts, for while the top staff in question do live in the Washington metropolitan area, they reside in what is normally called "suburban" rather than "urban" Washington: about 70 per cent of division chiefs (about thirty-five persons in all) live in such suburbs as Bethesda and Rockville, Maryland, and Arlington and McLean, Virginia. All but two of the rest live in far North West Washington, an area distinctly suburban in architecture, residential pattern, occupation, and socioeconomic class composition.

---

[1] Bureau chiefs, Executive Director, Assistant to the Chairman, General Counsel, chief of Hearing Examiners.

Ranking of Law Schools

The Statement accuses the authors of the Critique of charging "indirectly" that all graduates from other than "prestigious" law schools are "second-class lawyers coming from mediocre schools." The Critique made no such charge at all—either directly or indirectly; it criticized the Chairman and bureau chiefs for discriminating *against* graduates of recognized "national" law schools.[1]

The authors not only did not criticize the quality of young staff attorneys in the Critique, but explicitly praised their ability and enthusiasm, pointing out that many become understandably discouraged with the lack of effective leadership at the FTC and therefore (and very properly) leave to find some more vital agency in which to work.

Hiring of Negroes

The Statement takes issue with the Critique's conclusion that the FTC has hired few Negroes as attorneys. Mr. Dixon claims that since he has been Chairman he has made "a positive effort to attract and hire qualified

---

[1] The Chairman claims that offers of employment have nearly always been made to persons graduating in the upper 50 per cent of their class. This sort of wooden statistical approach is exactly what the Critique took issue with. It is not "arrogance" but simple and demonstrable fact —because of the existence of a nationwide and highly reliable test of legal aptitude (the Law School Admission Test)—that, for example, a person graduating in the 30th percentile from a highly ranked "national" law school will be a better lawyer than a person graduating in the same percentile from a lower-ranked school. The FTC's hiring formula should take this into account.

Negroes for attorney positions . . ." This assertion is contradicted by a top staff member involved in hiring personnel who unequivocally stated to the project's investigators that in the last few years the Chairman has shown absolutely no interest in hiring Negroes. This conclusion is corroborated for earlier years by the 1965 Civil Service Commission Report, which stated:

> The [FTC's] program for equal employment apparently has not been effectively implemented throughout the agency.

> Much greater effort must be made to seek out minority group candidates for professional positions. The system of almost total reliance on walk-ins must be replaced with a program of aggressive search.

Mr. Dixon claims that he has persuaded a total of ten Negroes to join the FTC as attorneys, of whom five (he says) are still so employed. Thus, by his own admission, the turnover rate among Negro attorneys at the FTC is 50 per cent, which gives some indication of a lack of sympathetic interest in encouraging professional employment for Negroes. Civil Service statistics reflect this backsliding: Since 1965, the number of Negroes in professional ranks at the FTC has declined from 0.98 per cent to 0.79 per cent, while Negro employment at comparable levels for all Federal agencies has climbed from 2.4 per cent to 3.0 per cent.

Finally, according to a written statement given to the authors by the FTC's Director of Personnel, only three of the five Negroes thought by Mr. Dixon to have been hired as attorneys are presently employed as attorneys. One is a textile investigator and one a librarian. In other words, Mr. Dixon's information about the program in which he claims to take such a personal interest is not very accurate.

Party Politics in Hiring and Advancement

The Statement claims that the Critique contains

unfounded false accusations with respect to political influences at the Federal Trade Commission. For instance, the report says that of the nearly 500 attorneys on the staff of the Commission that [sic] only about 40 are Republicans.

The Statement queries how the "Nader group" arrived at "this mystical figure of 40 Republicans." This figure was given to the authors by a reliable member of the staff at the Washington office who had drawn up the list in consultation with the one Republican bureau chief and another staff attorney. (All three compilers have been at the FTC more than fifteen years).[1]

The list, which appears in Section 15 of the Appendix, contains forty-two names, thirty-six of whom are persons in the central office (11 per cent of the 319 attorneys

---

[1] This allegation, which subsequent text shows to be well-founded, was only one of several well-founded cases of blatant party politics engaged in by the Chairman. Another was the Critique's allegation that the Chairman until recently openly solicited campaign funds from staff members at the Commission's central office in Washington. This charge has been fully substantiated through independent investigation by reporters as described in *The St. Louis Post-Dispatch*, January 6, 1969, p. 7A.

there). The source says there may be "a few" Republicans in field offices in addition to the six accounted for in the list. In other words, the numbers in the Critique are not "unfounded false accusations" but accurate descriptions of the politics of the FTC.

Civil Service Report Recommendations

The Statement contends that contrary to the allegations in the Critique, the Chairman has "adopted virtually all of the recommendations" made in the 1965 Civil Service Commission Report. Data in the Critique demonstrates that this claim is erroneous in substance. Thus, for example, the Report's recommendations about minority-group hiring for professional positions have not been carried out, as a comparison of the statistics for 1965 and 1968 illustrates.

The high turnover rate discussed above for the few Negro attorneys hired by the FTC indicates that a related recommendation of the Civil Service Commission Report has not been carried out either. The Civil Service Report suggested that the FTC initiate a program of education in "equal opportunity" among its (sometimes unsympathetic) staff. When 50 per cent of Negro attorneys hired leave the Commission, the inference is inescapable that no such education program has been carried out. Additional Civil Service Commission recommendations quoted in the Critique deal with violations of the Classification Act of 1949—creation of overlapping and conflicting employment positions (due in part to overly rapid advancement), use of high-grade attorneys for trivial tasks (such as answering nonlegal letters, monitoring), etc. The detailed evaluation of present FTC personnel structure contained in the Critique demonstrates that the flaws perceived by the Civil Service Commission in 1965 still exist; in other words, that the Chairman, as administrative officer, has taken no substantial steps to bring the agency into compliance with the Classification Act.[1]

Another section of the Civil Service Commission Report, quoted in the Critique, criticized the FTC's failure to make productive use of computers in its operations, and recommended that the Commission take steps to bring computers into full use in providing both "management" and "program resource" data. The project's computer expert discovered that while a small amount of rudimentary use has been made of computers in the personnel area, nothing has been done of any significance in the program resource area. In fact, the FTC has not even gone so far as to acquire adequate hardware for even the most minimal computerized operation.

Finally, the Civil Service Commission Report expressed concern over the FTC's shift to "voluntary" enforcement procedures, suggesting that what actually seemed to be occurring was an over-all decline of work (which had led to fear among staff attorneys that one day they would have no work to do!). The Civil Service Commission went so far as to recommend *abolishing* the Bureau of Industry Guidance, which is primarily re-

---

[1] Confidential discussions in December, 1968, with a member of the staff of the Civil Service Commission corroborate the findings of the Critique in this respect.

sponsible for administering the "voluntary" enforcement tools. Needless to say, the FTC has neither modified its "voluntary" approach nor abolished the Bureau of Industry Guidance since 1965.

Failure to Mention
Positive Accomplishments of FTC

The Statement ends with the complaint that the Critique failed to mention any "accomplishment by the Commission." That is true; what is more the authors agree that some of the matters cited in the Statement constitute palpable contributions by the FTC. However, the authors would not have had the material to match their comments with an equally strong account of positive contributions. They therefore intentionally focused on warranted criticisms and properly labeled the document a "Critique." There was also a more profound reason, however, for emphasizing the negative aspects of the FTC's consumer-protection record. This was done in an attempt to correct the agency's overly positive image, which, as the Critique documents, is the product of internal public relations, currying of Congressional favor, and business collusion.

Conclusion: Recommendations Reiterated ("The Cure")

In sum, the Chairman's Statement in no way weakens the thoroughly documented and carefully reasoned conclusions and recommendations set forth in the Critique.

In fact, these matters continue to demand swift and thorough public attention and Congressional action.

January 23, 1969

The Bar Association Report

The fight to reform the FTC has by no means ended with our report. However, there is no doubt that the report itself has produced some minor changes in the FTC's operations and sense of priorities. For example, the Commission has begun to open to public scrutiny secret deliberations with corporations that have disputed proposed complaints. This happened in two notable cases in the spring of 1969—one involved a proposed complaint against the Cox Broadcasting Corporation, the other a move to make Litton Industries divest itself of a German typewriter company.

When measured against our proposed reforms, however, these changes are small. The struggle, therefore, has moved into the arena of the Senate where, in April, 1969, we testified before Senator Abraham A. Ribicoff's Subcommittee on Executive Reorganization. After presenting prepared testimony that reiterated with additional examples the major points in our report, including tape-recorded samples of deceptive advertising that continues to defy FTC cease and desist orders, we were questioned by the Senators. The subjects covered were the serious problems of industry and advertising—such as motivational research, product differentiation, and product fixing—on which the FTC had failed to act aggressively. At the close of the hearing Senator Ribicoff stated:

> My feeling is that you gentlemen have accomplished something. I have got a hunch that your testimony and your report have shaken up the FTC, and I wouldn't be a bit surprised if some of their methods wouldn't undergo a change. I would hope so.[1]

Chairman Dixon was invited to respond to our charges, and on April 24, 1969, he appeared before the subcommittee. In his prepared testimony he stressed the antitrust work of the Commission (although he later admitted that 50 per cent of its resources are allocated to deceptive practices). He thereby avoided direct response to our charges. When the senators brought specific examples to his attention, he ambiguously referred them to lengthy case histories (in the matters of analgesics and Geritol), or he gave confused and garbled answers. His evasive reply to the charge of inaction in the case of Firestone's deceptive advertising led to the following exchange with Senator Ribicoff:

> Mr. Dixon: I have the head of the Deceptive Practices Bureau here, and I know that matter is receiving attention down below. . . . (W)e do have to look at it and we are looking at it.
> Senator Ribicoff: How complicated is it when someone advertises that their tire stops 25% quicker and they do

[1] Senate hearing held before the Subcommittee on Executive Reorganization to consider S. 860 Establishing a Department of Consumer Affairs, March 18, 1969, p. 156.

not say quicker than what or under what circumstances? Is this not easy for you to go into?

Mr. Dixon: If that was all we were going to look at, yes. But we are looking at them for several other things. We do not just look at this, that and the other thing. We have a whole series of things we are looking at, and it is merged into the problem. It is not just the fact of my picking up the telephone, perhaps, Senator, as you could and call the head of Firestone and say "Ha, you are saying this, what is your basis for it, do you have any tests? If you do not have any tests, why don't you stop it?"

Senator Ribicoff: Why don't you do it that way?

Mr. Dixon: We do that many times in many fields.

Senator Ribicoff: All right. Why could you not do it with Firestone?

Mr. Dixon: I do not know if this is true or not. I do not know what evidence they have submitted to us. I have looked at it. I know with the staff, it is being considered, sir.[1]

The most revealing testimony came at the end, when Chairman Dixon presented in a nutshell his "regulatory" philosophy, commenting on proposed consumer legislation:

Mr. Dixon: Now, you pass that kind of law and the lawyers will really applaud you the rest of their lives. But I will tell you that every businessman in the U.S. would be in court all day long, too.

Senator Ribicoff: Do you not find, though, that business can protect itself pretty well? They have counsel and lawyers. They can pay for them. You will find out in your project in Washington that these people who are being

---

[1] *Ibid.*, April 24, 1969, p. 451.

defrauded and cheated could never protect themselves. Who should protect them?

Mr. Dixon: Senator, that is the problem.[1]

Senator Ribicoff responded:

Senator Ribicoff: [I]n your whole statement, you do not seem to be very concerned about what your relationship should be relative to the consumer. You talk about mergers and how proud you are of all you have done in the antitrust field which you share with the Justice Department. But yet on the day-to-day problem of the consumer, there does not seem to be the same concern.

I do feel your agency has done a crusading job, outstanding, in the field of cigarette hazards. But I cannot find from anything you have testified, anything in any other field that would be comparable to it.[2]

Within days after we testified before Senator Ribicoff's subcommittee, the FTC announced intentions to engage in extensive monitoring of mass media. Our testimony had concentrated in this area. It had been very well-received by the subcommittee and was well covered by the Washington press. Shortly thereafter the FTC announced plans to proceed against Campbell's Soup for using marbles in their soup ads. The marbles cushioned the vegetables in the soup, making it appear richer than it was. This was just about as far as the FTC went in pursuing the "new campaign." Actually, Campbell's had previously agreed not to use the marbles. The FTC action is typical of the agency's response to public

[1] *Ibid.*, p. 485.

[2] *Ibid.*, pp. 484–486.

pressure. First, there is a grandstand announcement, then a few follow-up gestures, but in the end the matter quietly dies. Meanwhile, we were being congratulated for stirring up a somewhat senescent agency, and the agency was congratulated for responding constructively to criticism and for having the flexibility to mend its ways.

The original report also affected the internal machinery of the Commission. Apart from the increasing struggle for Republican favor between Chairman Dixon and Commissioner Jones, there have been signs of growing rebellion against the Chairman. Not only was there an attempt, though ill-fated, to remove hiring power from the hands of Mr. Dixon's friends, but also the Commission has recently voted seriously to inhibit the Chairman's promotion powers. The vote was three to one in favor of a curb, with Mr. Dixon against and Mr. MacIntyre abstaining. The new procedure would determine supergrade promotions not through the unchecked fiat of the Chairman (note the homogeneity of the present bureau heads), but through vote by the Commission as a whole. Commissioner Jones, who was then envisioning herself as the future Chairman, hesitated, but voted for the provision because she was convinced by the others that in giving the other Commissioners this power she would increase co-operation at the top and hence promote her own power. Mr. Dixon's personal power was still so great that a procedure such as this could do little to diminish it. For although a score of vacancies had already arisen within the agency's upper staff through retirement, death, etc., not a single one had been filled at the time of writing. Mr. Dixon was not about to cede control of this vital aspect of his power. And he did not have to, at least not at that time, for he was still able to assign his favored middle-level friends to assume upper-level duties unofficially. This is no great task for the GS-14 or 15 because under the present scheme there isn't very much to do at either level.

On April 21, 1969, the White House asked the American Bar Association to study and "make recommendations for the future activities and organization" of the Federal Trade Commission, requesting the report for early September. The first vacancy on the Commission was to occur on September 25. The Bar Association report is one that must be of crucial importance to the consumer, constituting a mandate for the new chairman of the FTC.

APPENDIX

1 A Brief Overview of the
Federal Trade Commission

Our criticism of the quality of the FTC's performance in consumer protection is based on certain assumptions about the agency's proper role—specifically that Congress has conceived of the FTC primarily as an enforcement agency rather than as a mere information-gathering or advice-giving agency. Further, Congress has over the last 30 years increasingly emphasized protection of *consumer* interests when prescribing the Commission's duties.

At its creation in 1914, the FTC was designed primarily to deal with *antitrust* problems—the Federal Trade Commission Act and the Clayton Act were considered together by Congress as extensive to the Sherman Antitrust Act. And under the FTC Act, Congress intended the FTC to perform several functions in connection with antitrust problems. These included data-gathering and informing businessmen (it was thought that the antitrust laws lacked "certainty," a deficiency that the FTC could remedy by advising businessmen on the legality of proposed business activities), as well as enforcement. Regarding enforcement, the Act provided specifically that

> The Commission is hereby empowered and directed to prevent persons, partnerships or corporations . . . from using unfair methods of competition in commerce
>
> § 5(a)(6) [1]

It went on to prescribe a form of procedure for establishing violations, halting them through the issuance of "cease and desist orders," and enforcing such orders by civil penalties. The structure of the original act suggests that, even at the

---

[1] All citations refer to the Federal Trade Commission Act.

outset, Congress intended the FTC's *major* responsibility to be that of enforcement, for that power is the first to be mentioned in the act.

The act's legislative history, however, has led some commentators to argue that the original intent of the Congress was to minimize the FTC's enforcement duties in favor of its legislative-investigative and business-advising roles. Some have jumped from that position to an assumption that the agency's enforcement responsibilities today should likewise be subordinated to the other functions. Such a view is erroneous as applied to the area of "direct consumer-protection," for it ignores the history of important later amendments to the FTC Act, including recent legislation. By "direct consumer-protection," we refer to the responsibility and authority to prevent consumer deception conferred on the FTC by certain key amendments to the FTC Act made in 1938 and expanded by later specialized statutes.

The background and legislative history of the relevant provisions of the Wheeler-Lea Act of 1938 demonstrate clearly that Congress intended by it to involve the FTC in direct consumer-protection and to give the agency an important and relevant *enforcement* role. In earlier years, the agency had occasionally taken halting steps toward involvement in direct consumer-protection enforcement by treating deception of consumers as one species of the "unfair methods of competition" proscribed in Section 5 of the FTC Act. In the *Raladam* case, however, the Supreme Court had held that evidence of consumer deception *alone* was insufficient to show a violation of the act. Congressional dissatisfaction with this holding, coupled with outrage and concern for the widespread and dangerous forms of consumer deception that sprang up in the Depression, led to the passage of the Wheeler-Lea Act. These circumstances alone suggest that Congress was primarily interested in having an *enforcement* agency—the FTC—to deal with consumer protection.

The specific provisions added to the FTC Act by the

Wheeler-Lea amendments and the legislative history of those amendments support such a view. For, not only did the amendments specifically outlaw "deceptive acts and practices," but they also gave the FTC new enforcement powers over particularly dangerous deception areas.[1] The Congressional discussion of the bill containing the amendments unambiguously emphasizes enforcement rather than aid to businessmen. This conception of the FTC as an enforcement agency has continued within the Congress to the present day, and is expressed in a series of specialized consumer-protection statutes.

The FTC's specific statutes include the Flammable Fabrics Act (which deals with practices dangerous to life and health) and three statutes [2] that regulate the labeling of textiles and furs (much less crucial than the Flammable Fabrics Act).[3]

The Commission's method of regulation is basically preventive; it seeks to discover, stop, and generally prevent practices that violate its laws. Paradoxically, while its powers of discovery are broad, its preventive powers are limited.

The FTC's information-gathering powers are set forth in Section 6 of the FTC Act:

(a)   To gather and compile information concerning, and to investigate from time to time, the organization, business, conduct, practices, and management of any corporation engaged in [interstate] commerce, excepting banks and common carriers . . . and its relation to other corporations and to individuals, associations, and partnerships.

(b)   To require, by general or special orders, corporations . . .

---

[1] The Commission was authorized to seek both criminal penalties and temporary injunctions to prevent deceptive advertising of foods, drugs, and cosmetics. (FTC Act, Sections 12, 14, and 15.)

[2] These are the Wool Products Labeling Act, the Fur Products Labeling Act, and the Textile Fiber Products Identification Act.

[3] The FTC also enforces the Truth in Packaging Act, the Insurance Act, etc. The former is not yet fully in effect; the latter, less important.

or any class of them . . . to file with the Commission in such form as the commission may prescribe annual or special, or both . . . , reports or answers in writing to specific questions, furnishing to the Commission such information as it may require as to the organization, business, conduct, practices, management . . . of the respective corporations . . .

Sections 9 and 10 compel compliance with Commission demands for information by providing for civil court enforcement under threat of contempt and for criminal sanctions for failure to respond or for false responses.

The only coercive legal enforcement tool generally available [1] to the FTC is the cease and desist order, which imposes no retroactive sanctions, but merely prohibits future repetition of the sort of conduct against which it is aimed. Once a cease and desist order becomes final (after 60 days or appeal to United States Courts of Appeals and the Supreme Court), it remains in effect permanently, and any violation may be punished by an action in the Courts of Appeals on behalf of the United States for recovery of "civil penalties" of up to $5,000 per day of violation.

Formal adjudicative proceedings leading to the issuance of cease and desist orders are prescribed by Section 5 of the FTC Act and the Commission's "Rules of Practice for Adjudicative Proceedings."

Whenever the Commission shall have reason to believe that . . . any . . . person, partnership, or corporation [subject to the FTC Act] has been or is using any . . . unfair or deceptive act or practice in commerce, and if it shall appear to the Commission that a proceeding by it in respect thereof would be to the interest of the public it shall issue and serve upon such person, partnership, or corporation a complaint stating its charges in that respect and containing a notice of a hearing

---

[1] In food and drug cases and under the textile and fur statutes, the Commission, in theory, has the additional powers to seek preliminary injunctions and even criminal penalties.

upon a day and at a place therein fixed at least thirty days after the service of said complaint. The person, partnership, or corporation so complained of shall have the right to appear at the place and time so fixed and show cause why an order should not be entered by the Commission requiring such person, partnership, or corporation to cease and desist from the violation of the law so charged in said complaint.

The "public-interest" requirement was written into the statute to allow the Commission to carry its enforcement program even beyond matters on which it has received citizen and merchant complaints.

FTC Rules also provide procedures for securing "consent" (non-contested) cease and desist orders without going through the adjudicatory process (hearing, initial decision, appeal, Commission decision) involved in regular cease and desist order cases.

The Federal Trade Commission uses several other enforcement techniques that do not lead to cease and desist orders (and thus cannot draw on the coercive powers underlying enforcement of cease and desist orders). Two of these are methods for dealing with entire industries rather than with individuals with regard to practices that investigation shows to be widespread; these proceedings lead to issuance of industry guides and trade-regulation rules. Two others deal with individual merchants: a means by which businessmen can solicit and receive "advisory opinions" on proposed courses of business action and a procedure for FTC acceptance of informal "assurances of voluntary compliance" in lieu of cease and desist orders.

The FTC staff at the principal office is divided into administrative offices and operating bureaus. The bureaus are structured along "program" rather than "functional" lines, that is, according to statutes or programs administered rather than the kinds of tasks performed by employees (as investigation, litigation, etc.). The major operating bureaus are those of Deceptive Practices, Economics, Field Operations, Industry Guidance, Restraint of Trade, and Textiles and Furs.

The major administrative offices are those of the Secretary, Program Review Officer, General Counsel, Hearing Examiners, and Executive Director (including Office of Administration).

The Commission itself is composed of five members appointed by the President, by and with the advice and consent of the Senate, for staggered seven-year terms. It has delegated some of its statutory authority to the chiefs of various operating bureaus. However, the over-all decision-making process of the Commission remains highly centralized, for no powers have been delegated to personnel beyond assistant bureau directors, all of whom are in the central office.

The Chairman, appointed by the President, has extensive powers and responsibility in the management of the FTC. He is its top administrative officer and is responsible for hiring and promoting persons on the staff.

2 *Enforcement Analysis* *

	Consent Orders	Cease and Desist Orders **	Textile and Fur *** Case or Matter Involving Country-of-Origin Protection for Business Interests	All Other Deceptive Practices
Last half of 1964	77	28	60	45
1965	75	27	49	53
1966	108	22	58	72
1967	106	32	78	60
Last half of 1968	72	15	41	46
Total	438	124	286	276
TOTAL ORDERS	562		562	

* Source: *FTC News Summary*
** Usually computed from initial-decision stage
*** Does not include flammable fabrics

3 Size Analysis

Litigated cases on docket first four months of 1968 *

	Restraint of Trade	Deceptive Practices	Total
1967 sales over 1 billion	2	0	2
1967 sales ½ billion to 1 billion	3	1	4
1967 sales 100 million to ½ billion	8	3	11
1967 sales ½ million to 100 million	8	0	8
Unlisted or *net worth* below 500 thousand	5	33	38

* Note that since this list includes only those companies able to delay enforcement through expensive litigation, it would consist of the largest companies. Those who submit to voluntary compliance, etc. are almost unanimously small.

4 Complaints Issued by the Commission *

Fiscal Year	1963	1964	1965	1966	1967	1968 **
Restraint of Trade	230	95	26	94	124	11
Deceptive Practices	129	129	66	48	108	27
Textiles and Furs	72	85	69	52	89	44
TOTAL	431	309	161	194	221	82

* Based on FTC Annual Reports
** Through third quarter

5 Completed Investigation Case Load *

Fiscal Year	1964	1965	1966	1967	1968 **
Restraint of Trade	467	729	492	321	139
Deceptive Practices	1090	981	981	737	422
TOTAL	1557	1710	1473	1058	561

* Based on FTC Annual Reports
** Through third quarter

6 Deceptive-Practice Cases
Avowed Applications for Complaint *

Fiscal Year	1961	1962	1963	1964	1965	1966	1967
Percentage investigated	30	19	25	23	19	14	11
Percentage resulting in issuance or approval of complaint	8	4	4	6	4	2	3

* Based on FTC Annual Reports

7 Cases Disposed of by Orders
to Cease and Desist *

Fiscal Year	1966	1967	1968 **
Consented	143	118	68
Contested	16	16	18
Admissive Answers and Defaults	2	5	2
TOTAL	161	139	88

* Partial orders excluded
** Through third quarter

8 Assurances of Voluntary Compliance

Fiscal Year	1966	1967	1968 *
	422	559	360

* Through third quarter

9 Total Civil Penalties, July, 1964–July, 1968

FTC News Summary	Area or Company	Damages
October 1, 1964	Vitasafe	$ 18,000
October 9, 1964	Davidson Vending	5,000
October 14, 1964	Time, Inc.	30,030
February 23, 1965	W. B. Saunders	20,000
April 5, 1965	American Candle Co.	1,500
April 28, 1965	McFadden-Bartell	35,500
November 4, 1965	Chun King	70,000
December 14, 1965	Americana	100,000
March 2, 1966	wool	30,000
June 4, 1966	fur	5,000
August 8, 1966	wool	20,000
August 8, 1966	flammable fabrics	35,000
December 16, 1966	flammable fabrics	10,000
February 2, 1967	flammable fabrics	12,000
May 6, 1967	wool	9,500
May 22, 1968	wool	15,000
	16 cases	$416,530

10 Personnel Increases

Year	Appropriation	Personnel	Approximate Number of Personnel necessary to keep even with GNP *
1962	$10,345,000	1,126	(from 1962)
1963	11,472,500	1,178	1,281
1964	12,214,000	1,144	1,351
1965	13,459,107	1,175	1,426
1966	13,500,000	1,145	1,506
1967	14,403,000	1,170	1,581
1968	15,281,000	1,230	1,671

* Other indices of appropriate FTC growth, including the merger-incidence rate, the growth of advertising, and the receipt of applications for complaint from the public generally far outstrip even the Gross National Product in expansion over this period.

11 Percentage of Black Employees *

	GS 9–18	GS 5–8	GS 1–4
June, 1965	0.98% (6 of 611)	11.0% (33 of 299)	24.6% (51 of 207)
June, 1966	1.28% (7 of 547)	9.5% (25 of 263)	34.5% (69 of 200)
November, 1967	0.78% (5 of 638)	12.0% (33 of 274)	42.6% (104 of 244)

* From *Study of Minority Group Employment in the Federal Government,* Civil Service Commission.

12 *Applicants and Appointments Offered by Region*

Class of '67	Per Cent of Total Applicants	Per Cent of Total Applicants Offered Appointment	Per Cent of Regional Applicants Offered Appointment
North	43	29	22
South	18	26	47
Midwest	25	30	38
Far West	15	15	33
	101 *	100	
Class of '68			
North	49	35	17
South	17	28	37
Midwest	26	29	25
Far West	8	9	26
	100	101 *	

* Figures exceed 100 per cent because of rounding off.

13 Legal Aptitude and Law-School Standing

	Aver. Honor Code No.*		Size of Sample	
	North	South	North	South
1968 all applicants	4.6	4.2	(203)	(49)
1968 offered appointments	3.5	3.6	(35)	(28)

	Aver. LSAT Score			
	North	South		
1968 all applicants	574	597	(143)	(47)
1968 offered appointments	596	571	(22)	(16)
1967 all applicants	569	550	(90)	(34)
1967 offered appointments	534	541	(14)	(14)

* Indicates applicants were on the average in second 25 per cent of class.

14 Selected Law Schools and Appointments Offered

Law Schools	Offered Appointment	Refused Appointment	Total	Per Cent Offered Appointment
New York University	3	31	34	9%
Georgetown University	4	11	15	27%
University of Texas	5	9	14	36%
George Washington University	14	19	33	42%
St. John's University	6	40	46	13%
University of Kentucky	9	2	11	82%
Brooklyn Law School	6	38	44	14%
University of Tennessee	6	10	16	38%

	2 Yr. Combined LSAT Aver. of Applicants	Size of Sample	'68 Aver. Honor Code No.	Size of Sample
New York University	612	(19)	4.9	(20)
Georgetown University	591	(14)	4.7	(6)
University of Texas	588	(3)	4.7	(10)
George Washington University	569	(12)	3.9	(18)
St. John's University	565	(37)	5.8	(28)
University of Kentucky	558	(5)	3.1	(7)
Brooklyn Law School	554	(24)	4.0	(17)
University of Tennessee	525	(7)	3.9	(13)

15 Republicans on FTC Staff as of August, 1968

Name	Bureau *
Charles Moore	Field Operations
David R. Refl	DP
Raymond L. Hays, Jr.	RT
Basil J. Mezines	RT
John T. Walker	DP
Donald A. Surine	RT
Bernard Williamson	RT
Kathryn P. Casey	DP
Janet D. Saxon	DP
Emerson K. Elkins	GC
Henry G. Pons	DP
Charles T. MacDonald	GC
Arthur R. Woods, Jr.	IG
Paul A. Jamarik	IG
Michael P. Hughes	TF
Edward B. Finch	TF
William A. Somers	DP
Charles W. O'Connell	DP
Thomas G. Egan	IG
Richard B. Mathias	RT
Daniel H. Hanscom	GC
Keith Q. Hayes	FO (Kansas City)
Simen F. House	FO (Washington Area)
Lynn M. Hubler	GC
Daniel R. Kane	RT
Richard B. McMahill	IG
Robert E. Freer, Jr.	DP
Harold D. Rhynedance, Jr.	GC
Paul C. Steinbach	IG

* DP = Deceptive Practices, RT = Restraint of Trade, GC = General Counsel's Office, IG = Industry Guidance, TF = Textiles and Furs, FO = Field Office, AA = Attorney Adviser to Commissioner MacIntyre

15 Republicans on FTC Staff as of August, 1968 (cont'd)

Name	Bureau *
Vernon E. Taylor	FO (Cleveland)
John G. Underwood	DP
Theodor P. von Brand	AA
Joachim J. Volhard	AA
Franklin P. Michels	AA
Frank M. Whiting	DP
Roslyn D. Young, Jr.	RT
Edmund D. Mulville	RT
John Grey	FO (Washington Area)
Charles F. Simon	DP
William D. Dixon	IG
Charles T. Snavely	FO (Kansas City)
Frederick Lukens	FO (Seattle)

INDEX

INDEX

DATE DUE